TEACHERS' MANUAL

WORKBOOK IN SECOND LANGUAGE ACQUISITION

Larry Selinker   Susan Gass

University of Michigan

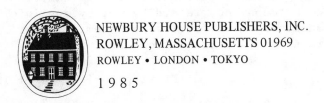

NEWBURY HOUSE PUBLISHERS, INC.
ROWLEY, MASSACHUSETTS 01969
ROWLEY • LONDON • TOKYO

1 9 8 5

Library of Congress Cataloging in
  Publication Data

Selinker, Larry, 1937-
  Workbook in second language acquisition.

  1. Language acquisition. 2. Language and
languages--Study and teaching. I. Gass,
Susan M. II. Title.
P118.S39 1985   418'.007   85-296
ISBN 0-88377-293-0

NEWBURY HOUSE PUBLISHERS, INC.

  Language Science
  Language Teaching
  Language Learning

ROWLEY, MASSACHUSETTS 01969
ROWLEY • LONDON • TOKYO

                    First printing: April 1985
Printed in the U.S.A.   5   4   3   2   1

The decision to write a <u>Teachers' Manual</u> to accompany <u>Workbook in Second Language Acquisition (Workbook)</u> was not an easy one. On the one hand, we recognize the need to provide guidelines for a <u>Workbook</u> of this sort. On the other hand, we are aware of the fact that <u>good</u> L2 research involves more than just answering questions about data; good argumentation is crucial to the research process. Data are often ambiguous and by themselves do not provide explanations. It is the analyst who provides explanations by means of organization, reorganization, interrelations, additional data analysis, reanalysis, argumentation, and so forth. These are the abilities which we hope will be developed in the student as a result of carefully working through the problems in the <u>Workbook</u>.

Argumentation in L2 acquisition is not an easy process to teach. Throughout this manual we have attempted to provide information on what counts as evidence for and against a particular analysis and how one can deal with putative counter-examples (cf. Problem 4.3 for an example).

The questions are ordered in such a way that they take students from the data to an analysis step by step. Teachers may wish to make explicit to students what is implicit in

the ordering of questions. The following two
examples of problems show precisely what is intended and how the process of analysis can be
made explicit to students. Note that within
the context of the Workbook the research question is defined by the problem itself. Defin-
ing a research question is, of course, a
necessary and important step in research.
Consider Problem 5.1. The research question
is "What functions do the past and present
tenses serve in a narrative for this L2
learner?" Given the narrative in this problem,
the first step is to separate the examples of
present and past tense so that one can focus on
the function of each one. Separation of this
sort may not always be straightforward since it
is not clear how one should categorize modals
(cf. "couldn't," line 15), for example. The
procedure we suggest in this problem is one of
separate columns. Some students seem to function better highlighting the examples in two
colors. After the data are separated, one next
looks for patterning in the data to explain the
shift. Question five then takes the students
from individual analyses of spoken and written
data to a comparison of the samples. In looking at the similarities and differences and
accounting for them, students are instructed to
be specific (provide examples) and to appeal to
external sources (in this case data from a
different problem) to support their analyses
and interpretation. These are steps one could
take in one's own research: determine a research question, look at relevant data, search
for generalizations to account for the results,
provide specific examples, and appeal to other
sources (other results reported in the literature).

Problem 4.4 (particularly Part I) can also
be used to help make explicit the process of
argumentation. In this case the focus is on
longitudinal development of question formation.
The first step is to order the data sequen-
tially and then compare the two data sets. In
this problem it is, in fact, the difference in
question formation which allows one to understand the appropriate IL generalization the
child was making at an earlier stage.

In some cases two questions approach the
data from different perspectives. For example,
in Problem 8.2 the first three questions aim at
an understanding of variables which were and
were not controlled for. In particular, question 1 aims indirectly at the question of the
interpretation of results, whereas question 3
aims more directly at the same point. This is
done in order to make it easier for students to
come up with an analysis. It is, of course,
possible for teachers to combine questions or
to omit a question. Similarly, teachers may
wish to add or change a question to emphasize
a different part of the analysis than we did.
We would like to hear from teachers about
alternatives which seem to work better.

Because we feel that in many cases there
are a number of possible answers, some perhaps
more plausible than others, we would like the
users of this Workbook to realize that this
Teachers' Manual is intended only as a guide to
issues and discussion rather than as a presenta-
tion of the correct answer. We further hope
that the limited data that are presented in
each problem will enable students of second
language acquisition to consider what might be

confirming/disconfirming evidence for the specific hypotheses that have been created in each
case.

For each problem we present a possible
answer(s) and in many cases point out issues
which are raised by the data in that problem.
We intend these issues to form an integral part
of the class discussion which we hope will
arise from working through individual problems.

In addition to colleagues thanked in the
Workbook, we would like to thank those participants of the "All India Seminar on Interlanguage," Hyderabad, February 1983, for patiently
helping to talk through possible solutions to
some of the problems in the Workbook. We would
additionally like to thank several colleagues
who helped with solutions to individual problems: Josh Ard, Ellen Broselow, Moira
Chimombo, Edith Hanania, and Benji Wald.
References that appear in the Workbook are not
repeated in this Manual. Additionally, abbre-
viations used here appear on p. vi of the
Workbook.

Larry Selinker   Susan Gass

Ann Arbor
November 1984

CONTENTS (continued)

PROBLEM 1.1

These data come from compositions written
in English by Polish learners. For examples
such as those in Part I, Arabski (1979:88)
states that "the -ing form is used as an over-
extended morphological form," i.e., there appears to be a consistency in the IL in that the
learner is consistently "replacing" expected 0
in the TL with the -ing ending. Arabski further claims that the learner in this case had
reached what Corder (1973:131) has called the
"systematic stage" of IL development. This
systematicity is shown in a statistical sense
by observing in the data whether "they are
typical or not." The data in Part II present
a different case, "the presystematic stage
where the substitutions are not systematic."
The influence of the phrasing of the question
"Why I wouldn't like to get married before I
finish my studies," however, seems evident in
the learner data (see Problem 4.9) and appears
to make the data more systematic than it probably is. Not once in the data of Part II, for
example, do the learners "break" the string
get married, so it is conceivable that it is
seen as a unit. There is no direct evidence
as to whether or not the unit is analyzed. One
might suppose, however, that there has been
some analysis for the following reasons:
1) the form is written so the learners can see
a word break and 2) the learners are fairly
sophisticated so that one can assume that the
individual words get and married are known to
them. In fact, married is used in the data
without get. With regard to other constructions, one notes some target-like consistency
due to the influence of the question:

Sentence 1: <u>wount to go</u>, <u>wount to do</u>;
Sentence 2: <u>going to do</u>;
Sentence 3: <u>want to go</u>; and
Sentence 4: <u>want to do</u>.

However, this is not true in all cases. In sentence 3, <u>when I'll graduation</u> = <u>when I graduate</u> and <u>I wouldn't to get married</u> = <u>I won't get married</u>. This is particularly interesting since the apparent influence of the question on the IL data appears to create a morphological error in tense sequencing. There appears to be target-like consistency in these learners' use of the modal <u>must</u>:

Sentence 7: <u>must finish</u>;
Sentence 11: <u>must be</u>;
Sentence 12: <u>must finish</u>; and
Sentence 15: <u>must make</u>.

The verb form <u>is</u> appears to be the form of preference for present tense generic meaning:

Sentence 5: <u>married is</u>;
Sentence 10: <u>18 years is</u>; and
Sentence 14: <u>men 18 years old is</u>.

In Part II in comparison with Part I, one finds a variety of forms. One possibility for viewing these data would make Part II learners more advanced because of this variety and the apparent "hypothesis testing." Another possibility would make Part I learners more advanced because of the apparent systematicity of using -<u>ing</u> for many constructions. The latter view could be related to phenomenon of "U-shaped learning" (Kellerman, 1985) where apparent errors, when systematic, represent a step forward in the analysis of the target language system.

In general terms, learners appear to be
able to access a root of a word, but often appear unable to access the "correct" (TL)
morphological ending in the appropriate context (cf. Problem 2.1).

PROBLEM 1.2

English-like	Non-English-like
1,5,6,8,10,12,	2,3,4,7,9,11,13,17,19
14 (how many ... years),	
15,16,18	

A possible IL generalization is that there
are no plural markers in phrases with quantify-
ing words (one counter-example is sentence 14
and possibly 10). Plural markers occur with
numbers and where there is a single noun (one
counter-example is seen in 11). An important
point to consider in this problem is a methodological one: if one is trying to attempt to
understand an individual's IL generalization,
then one must only consider that individual's
utterances. On the other hand, if one is using
pooled data, as is the case in this problem,
then it is to be expected that counter-examples
will abound (see also Problems 1.8 and 1.10).

PROBLEM 1.3

These data come from a 68-year-old man who
has lived in the U.S. for 31 years. Thus, he
can hardly be called a "learner" whose IL com-
petence is "transitional" (Corder 1981). He
is clearly a "fossilized" speaker of this IL
(Selinker 1972), whose English is not expected

to change, except for the possible addition of
lexical items. So one would expect his IL to
be the same at a later point in time.

The fact that 80 of his 85 negatives were
formed with no and 5 with not is interesting,
but with so little data simple statistical conclusions are to be handled with care. Sauzier
(1979:2) says that 4 of the 5 utterances with
not consist of not + phrase (nonverbal element):

    not too much
    not too mucha
    no, not it
    not too good

Number 4 in Part II not eate sugar is not + V.
However, this appears to be an abberation
since the overwhelming majority of cases of
the use of no involve the structure no + V
(1-10 of Part I) and the rest he classifies as
no + phrase (11-17). Note that in the case of
not eate there is a vowel following the negative element, whereas in the other examples of
no + verb a consonant follows the negative
(except in the case of number 5 which is an NL
not a TL form). In other words, as appears to
be the case in IL, there may be some non-TL
phonological conditioning in addition to syntactic conditioning in this subject's use of
no versus not. However, this distinction
cannot be discerned from the data in the problem. Sauzier (1979) claims that no good does
not function as no + phrase, but as a single
chunked unit, "as an adjective with the meaning
of bad." This speculation can lead to class
discussion on the possibility of "chunked" or
"unanalyzed units" in IL and can serve as an
introduction to problems 1.4, 4.4, and 4.6,
where this concept is raised more explicitly.

Sauzier treats "I don't know" (as does Schumann, Problem 1.10) as a "chunked unit," not affecting the production pattern no + V. The open question posed by the data involves no + phrase vs. not + phrase. Sauzier unfortunately presents little information here. One possibility is that no occurs before nouns and not before pronouns. Another is that not is the negative form before too. Still another possibility is that not precedes [t] or vowels. The one exception is number 11, although the [n] may have been syllabic. Class discussion can focus on the ambiguity apparent in these data and in L2 data in general.

Sauzier concludes with an important point about IL's in general: "He [the learner] has developed his IL in such a way that he can express a variety of sophisticated ideas and thoughts, albeit in a seemingly simplified syntax."

PROBLEM 1.4

The data for this problem come from a dissertation by Edith Hanania. Some of the results were published in Hanania and Gradman (1977).

The subject of the study was a 19- to 20-year-old Saudi wife and mother acquiring English in an untutored environment. During the period of data collection (18 months), her exposure to English was limited. The data come from a longitudinal study of this learner's English IL. Data were collected once monthly and were grouped into six three-month periods.

The data in this problem, taken from the learner's early development, relate to her

developing rule system for negation. A progression can be seen from the holophrastic no
and no preceding a noun to not (preceding an
adverb or V-ing) to don't as an imperative and
can't used somewhat productively as a negative
element within a sentence.

At Time 2, it is reasonable to assume that
can't was used as an unanalyzed routine. The
sentence in which it is used here is one which
is often used by NNS's as an apparent excuse
for not being able to successfully engage in a
conversation. Furthermore, the grammatical
knowledge necessary to productively use can't
exceeds this learner's ability since at the
same time she is using no and not as generalized negative forms.

Similarly, don't touch in the third period
may also be an unanalyzed unit. By Time 4
can't and don't are extended to new contexts.
Importantly, this may be taken as evidence for
their incorporation at this point into her rule
system for negation. This concept (cf. Corder
1981) is repeatedly seen throughout the
Workbook.

These data point to the need to distinguish between forms which are learned routines
(also referred to as "formulae," "chunks,"
[unanalyzed] units) and those which result
from a creative process. The distinction is
not always an easy one to make. This can be
the focus of discussion pointing out that
reference to other forms is necessary (e.g.,
the extension to new contexts, level of complexity of other forms in the learner's
grammar).

The data for this problem come from an
11-year-old female native Spanish speaker who
has been in the United States since age seven.
The object of analysis is her acquisition of
the form don't and doesn't. This problem
illustrates the difficulties in using an error
analysis perspective in analyzing L2 data.
Error analysis uses the standard L2 forms as
a basis of contrast and, as such, limits the
researcher to deviations from those norms,
rather than allowing him/her to understand the
system that the learner is using (cf. also
Problem 8.1). In this problem the distinction
between TL system and learner system is emphasized.

The learner appears to use don't as a
"present" or "habitual present" tense marker
and doesn't as a "past" tense marker. A
possible way of determining whether or not this
is the correct IL analysis would be to elicit
positive forms of do and does. This would
indicate whether the analysis should be limited
to her negative forms. One would also want to
gather data from other verbs (see sentence 3
and her use of was) to determine the limits of
this usage. Finally, one would want to analyze
her use of did and didn't.

In 1 in Part II, there is some evidence
that she analyzes does as the past tense of do.
At this point she does not have full English-
like control over third singular agreement for
the present, nor the irregular third singular
does as part of that paradigm. The final
example suggests the following IL system:

	POS	NEG
PRES	do	don't
PAST	did	doesn't

If this is in fact the case, it lends evidence
to the original view of the IL hypothesis
(Selinker 1972) of IL as a system, at least
partially different from the NL and the TL;
this possibility could be a source of useful
class discussion.

PROBLEM 1.6

The data source for this problem is the
same as that for Problem 1.4. In this case,
however, the object of analysis is the
learner's use of the progressive. In sentences
1-5, which consist of a single-word subject +
intransitive verb, the progressive form is
comprised of a form of the verb to be + V-ing.
In 6, where the subject of an SV sentence con-
sists of Determiner + N, only the V-ing element
of the progressive appears. In 7, which con-
sists of subject + transitive verb + object
(SVO), neither element of the progressive form
appears. In 8-10 which are also SVO sentences,
but which have an implied subject, the progressive is again not realized. A possible
explanation is that there are processing
constraints which only permit full progressive
forms with the simplest (SV) structures.
Another possible explanation is that the
learner only uses the full progressive when the
verb is the final element in the sentence.
This may be related to a distinction between
transitive and intransitive verbs (depending on
one's analysis of eat). A final point to note

and one which can be focussed on in class discussion is that the acquisition of a grammatical
form is variable, appearing in different environments at different times (cf. also Problems
4.4 and 4.7).

<u>PROBLEM 1.7</u>

This is the same group of learners as in
Problem 1.2. The use of prepositions in Part
I is clearly non-English-like, since in every
case we presumably would want to assign a
different structure from the point of view of
the TL:

1. from Morocco to Saudi Arabia
2. There are many ways ...
3. It is quite different ... [assumes
    this is a translation of the
    intention of the learner]
4. in Ann Arbor
5. for a long time
6. a month ago
7. He will finish his studies.
8. on this planet
9. with the housework
10. the Red Sea on the east

From individual data, one might be able to
determine if some sort of generalization is at
work, such as "use <u>from</u> for geographical locations." If this is the case, example 1 provides
a case of English-like behavior by chance (cf.
Corder 1981). A suggestion that could provide
fruitful class discussion is to have students
formulate a hypothesis of this sort and design
a way to test it.

Part II appears to provide a simplifying case as well; no preposition is provided where one is expected in the TL. This is a dangerous generalization (Corder 1983) for how can one "simplify" what one does not yet know. However, a learner can clearly realize that s/he doesn't know how to use prepositions appropriately in English and adopt a strategy "use no prepositions except in specifically constrained instances." Expected English prepositions are:

1. in British English
2. for the future
3. on his thesis
4. in the fall
5. this time (this may be another instance of correct TL behavior by chance)
6. out of Jeddah
7. for you

Number 7 might be a different case since a preposition dependent on a verb in the TL is involved. Whether IL works in this way is open to question (Jain 1969 and 1974) and this is one way IL's may be different from "natural" languages (cf. Adjemian 1976).

A reasonable answer for question 3, and this can lead to useful class discussions, is that no IL generalization is possible for the data in Part II, though a TL generalization from the point of view of error analysis is, in fact, possible: prepositions are omitted in adverbial phrases. In comparing Parts I and II, we see that it is easier to make possible IL generalizations with the presence of items as opposed to their absence. One can here discuss the advantages/disadvantages of error analysis (EA) vs. IL analysis. One could

compare (2) in Part II with the time expressions in Part I, and (6) in Part II with the
place expressions in I. For example, not using
the of in (6) but having a locative expression
out does not negate the inclusion of a locative
preposition for locative phrases. As is often
the case with a limited data set, there are not
enough exemplars to be more certain than that.

Part III presents correct TL forms. The
place expressions in Egypt, in Dallas, in this
area would negate the simple hypothesis of
using from for geographical locations, but the
learners may have made a distinction between
direction and location. There are two final
points to emphasize: 1) when attempting to
determine IL hypotheses, one should consider
individuals as well as groups, and 2) one must
be clear about intended meanings of learners
(Corder 1981) since what appears to have one
meaning in the TL may really have a different
meaning in IL (see also Problem 8.1).

PROBLEM 1.8

These data are from a study of French-
immersion children in Canada. The results
suggest randomness in terms of gender assignment. This is the case in the data with
natural gender (examples 2 and 3), as well
as with inanimate objects (mon lit vs. ma
lit). This problem points out a difficulty in
drawing conclusions about L2 grammars based
on grouped data (see also Problems 1.2 and
1.10). Unless it is the same child who
uttered mon lit and ma lit, one cannot be
sure whether gender assignment is random or
systematic.

The data from Part II show that, unlike the apparent randomness of Part I, there seems to be a pattern followed by these children: unless there is evidence to the contrary (such as natural gender, knowledge about the L2, etc.), mark a noun masculine. By Time 2 more of the gender assignments have been sorted out and most nouns are marked with the correct L2 gender.

In Part III, results are presented individual by individual. The trend is similar to that discussed thus far. For a discussion of overgeneralization of masculine/feminine pronoun usage, the reader is referred to Zobl (1985) who also uses French data, but in a different Canadian setting.

In general, percentage results are limited in that one doesn't have available raw data results. Thus 1/1 is given the same weight as 50/50. In these data, however, note that less than five tokens was not counted.

Within the context of this problem, one can discuss Contrastive Analysis (CA). It is not clear what an accurate CA prediction would be in this case. For example, one could predict that errors would not occur with human referents since English distinguishes between masculine and feminine in pronominal referents. However, gender in English is not marked on determiners. Thus, on the basis of one aspect of the gender system, one prediction would result; and, on the basis of another aspect, a different prediction would result. Thus, in this problem one can discuss the advantages/disadvantages of three approaches, EA, CA, and IL.

<u>PROBLEM 1.9</u>

These data come from responses to a
standard test of English language proficiency.
The main concern here is order of acquisition.
Learner C appears to be the most advanced
learner because all the forms used are standard L2 forms, with the exception of the past
participle in 3. B and D appear the least
advanced. B has only acquired the past tense
of <u>eat</u> and D, the auxiliary category for the
conditional, although not the tense or perfect
form. In general, learning the past tense of
<u>eat</u> and the use of an auxiliary in the plu-
perfect conditional appear to be the earliest
learned. On the other hand, the latest-
learned form seems to be the past participle
and the use of the perfect of the auxiliary
(modal + <u>have</u>). Learning the past of the
auxiliary is an intermediate structure, and
the past of <u>fall</u> and third singular verb
agreement are learned later than the past
auxiliary. Thus, one can see that there are
limits to doing order of acquisition analysis
since this sort of analysis is not absolute.
Rather, order of acquisition is a complex of
many factors, and class discussion can try to
ferret these out. In this problem one can
see that there is overlap in the acquisition
of the irregular pasts with the past conditional and with the third singular agreement
marker. There also appear to be multiple
stages in the acquisition of the pluperfect
conditional. This is similar to the "all or
nothing" phenomenon discussed in Problems
4.4 and 4.7.

PROBLEM 1.10

This problem concerns perhaps the most famous informant in the L2 literature, Alberto — a fossilized speaker. In Schumann (1978) are presented details of Alberto's situation in the United States as well as information about the data-gathering and data-analysis techniques which Schumann used. However, it is to be noted that Schumann does not describe negatives (the focus of this problem), but uses the negation context as one of his linguistic environments to study auxiliary forms. As Schumann points out, in order to understand the data, one has to separate formulas such as "I don't know" and "I don't understand" from other data (see Problem 1.3). This leads to an important point in L2 research: one must count tokens with a type. The tables and charts in Schumann (1978) are easily usable by the instructor and can be brought into the classroom discussion. Schumann's claim is that "aux's" do not vary for positive, negative, and interrogative sentences. Thus, he pools the data. This provides another opportunity for discussing the vexing question of pooling of data (see Problems 1.2 and 1.8).

Another point of discussion which arises from this problem is "morpheme order" and "obligatory contexts." One could include a discussion of the origin of these concepts (i.e., child language studies), why they were deemed useful for L2 research (Dulay and Burt 1974; and Bailey, Madden, and Krashen 1974) and the attacks on these concepts (Tarone 1974, Rosansky 1976).

These data (including those presented in Appendix I) are useful for having students

begin to look at large numbers of exemplars,
for learner variation, for investigator bias,
for longitudinal effects, for task variation
(see, in particular, Problems 3.4, 8.4, and
8.5), for coding decisions, for the necessity
of contextual information, and for the minutiae
of detail.

In terms of the longitudinal question,
interestingly, there appears to be no change in
Alberto's negative structures over time, which
is what one would expect from a speaker of
Alberto's background. The most common productive rule seems to be <u>no</u> + V. Concerning the
auxiliary structures:

<u>do</u>: Should one treat <u>don't remember</u>
      the same as one treats <u>don't</u>
      <u>understand</u>? If so, are they ex-
      amples of a productive use of
      negation or of chunked learning?
      One piece of evidence which sug-
      gests that they are examples of
      productive use is that both vary
      with <u>no + understand/remember</u>
      forms. In addition, <u>don't</u> is
      used with other verbs (<u>have</u>,
      <u>talk</u>, <u>see</u>).

<u>is</u>: occurs as <u>no is</u> and <u>is a</u>, typical
      pidgin-like IL sentences, and the
      seemingly correct <u>this isn't</u>.

modals: the only modal in the data is
        <u>can</u> which occurs relatively early
        as well as later in the data in the
        combination <u>don't can</u>. Also,
        one example of the productive rule
        <u>no + V</u> occurs with a modal <u>no can</u>
        <u>make</u>.

The boldface words all have the same root
as the correct TL words, but have different
affixes, e.g., discuss + ∅ vs. discuss + ion;
eas + y vs. eas + ily; scien + ce vs. scien +
tist. This is also true for the pair life -
live, although it is harder to segment the
words based on the orthography.

The IL forms are all shorter (or as short
as) the TL forms. Generally, the IL forms
seem to be semantically and morphologically
simpler, although determining simpler forms is
not a straightforward issue. A class discussion could ensue on this point.

In Part II the IL forms are again shorter
than the TL forms. All of the IL forms represent basic TL stems (possibly with a plural
marker), while in all cases except belief-
believe the correct TL forms have a suffix.

In Part III the IL forms are all longer
than the comparable TL forms, thus the generalization that learners select a shorter TL
form of morphologically related words does not
hold. One can comment here that in the spoken
data, the examples do point to a tendency to
select shorter forms, but in the written data,
both longer and shorter forms are selected.

In these data the learners appear to access
a member of a class (e.g., differ, differed,
differing, different) (although not always the
shortest or most basic), but appear unable to
determine the correct member of the TL class.
Selecting one basic form for use in other
contexts can also be seen in Problem 2.2.
One might want to consider whether a given

learner always selects a similar member from a
root class (shortest, most basic, etc.). What
are the relationships in frequency of the IL
form and the correct TL form? What in the
surrounding context would motivate the IL form?

PROBLEM 2.2

This problem deals directly with the issue
of simplification. In sentences 1 - 5 the
learners use the infinitive as the general verb
form. In Part II, #2, there is an additional
example of learners using a single form (ne pas
or n'est pas) to cover one semantic area, in
this case the negative. In #3, the infinitive
is used inappropriately. Not only is this a
potential example of simplification related to
the examples in 1 - 5, but one can also interpret these utterances as examples of language
transfer since the translation equivalents are
similar to comparable utterances in the NL.
Thus, this problem raises the issue of multiple
explanations of L2 data (see Problem 8.7) and
the ways one can (or cannot) distinguish
between them.

PROBLEM 2.3

Word meaning, possible hypotheses:

1. counting the word time
2. generalizing the word tall to a
   new context
3. same as 2 with the word big
4. same as 2 with the word close
5. same as 2 with the word graduate

6. appropriate usage in terms of the TL
7. take is used here with the meaning
    of receive, i.e., uses an appropri-
    ate word in terms of the semantics,
    rather than the more TL idiomatic
    expression get a ticket
8. appropriate usage in terms of the TL
9. possibly a NL usage. The learner
    uses two descriptive words, sweet
    and pastry, where standard English
    uses one (dessert). There is an
    additional problem in that the
    article is omitted which would have
    indicated the function the food
    served (dessert) rather than a
    description of its taste.
10. the learner generalizes the semantic
    concept of first to an environment
    in which standard English uses
    from the beginning
11. the semantic association is appar-
    ent here in that appreciate and
    value cover a similar range
12. another example of semantic associa-
    tion. The learner has apparently
    not yet learned the syntactic slot
    in which expensive fits.

The TL interpretations and correspondences
given above are the most obvious ones, but one
cannot know for sure whether they are the
meanings intended by the learner. It is possible there are IL sentences that seem "correct"
syntactically and contextually, but do not
convey the intended IL meanings (Corder 1981,
within the framework of EA calls these "covert
errors"). Two IL strategies are apparent
here: that of generalizing words to new
contexts and semantic association, where one

aspect of a word is generalized, taking on the
total meaning range for that word.

One would like to know the semantic limits
of the generalizations that learners can come up
with. For example, what is it about the word
graduate (leave a high school/college after
some academic achievement) that the learner
knows which allows him/her to extend it to the
environment in sentence 5? Are semantic features learned one by one? Would this same
speaker, for example, feel s/he graduates from
his/her house every day? If not, what are the
restrictions of generalizations? Is there a
minimum set of features which are learned along
with lexical items?

PROBLEM 2.4

These data are from the same French immersion program that students discussed in
Problems 1.8 and 2.2. In Part I the learners
appear to have transferred lexical meaning and
usage from their L1 to the L2. For example, in
1, the child uses the verb marcher, an intransitive verb, as a transitive verb. In 2, there
is an attempt to directly translate sometimes.
Des is a partitive which at times can be
translated as some, although in the context of
sometimes it does not have a partitive meaning.
Temps and times, while orthographically similar,
have different meaning ranges in the L1 and the
L2. Sentence 3, it is claimed (see references
for original problem), is an example of lexical
transfer. What is interesting is that the
translation equivalent of Il est trois ans, the
IL sentence, is not grammatical in the child's

NL, English. The child appears to recognize
that the translation equivalent of old is
inappropriate in French. (See, in this
regard, Problem 2.7 in which the issue of
translatable/transferrable items is raised
as a function of the learner's perception of
language specific and language universal
facts.) In 5, regarder has the meaning of
look at, not look in the sense of resemble,
as is used here. Thus, what is apparently
transferred is the extension of the verb in
a case where a connection between the NL and
TL primary meanings of a verb has been made.
In other words, we see an extension of the
semantic range to correspond to NL use.
Examples 6 and 7 show translation in progress
where the learner uses the lexical and
syntactic form of the NL, as well as a
familiar lexical form from the TL. In
sentence 8, the learner transfers the NL
meaning, some, which s/he most likely sees
as primary, to contexts which are allowed by
the NL, but not the TL.

The sentences in Part II illustrate
transfer of word order strategies, in that
in all instances the IL structures reflect
elements of NL word order (see also Problem
2.5).

PROBLEM 2.5

This problem deals with (over)generaliza-
tion of TL material. In 1 we hypothesize
that learners have taken the general N +
adjective pattern which exists in French and
extended it to an adjective which, in standard French, precedes the noun.

There are at least two explanations for the
pattern found in #2. First, it can be interpreted as the transfer of word order from the
L1. Second, it can be interpreted as an
extension of the subject pronoun to a position
which requires an oblique case pronoun. Class
discussion could revolve around questions such
as: How could one decide this issue? Could
it in fact be decided?

Sentence 3 shows the opposite pattern — an
object pronoun is used as a subject.

Finally, in sentence 4 the reflexive verb
which in standard French requires conjugation
with être, "to be," is conjugated with the
more common avoir, "to have."

Problems 2.4 and 2.5 differ in that one
shows a reliance on NL information and the
other on previously learned TL information.
What is similar is that, while they differ as
to the source of the information, both data
sets show the use and integration of prior
linguistic knowledge in L2 acquisition. In
class discussion one can devote time to a consideration of definitions of prior linguistic
knowledge and how that might (or might not)
differ from language transfer.

PROBLEM 2.6

There are at least two possible approaches
to these data, one more abstract than the
other. In the abstract approach, the learners
are assumed to be applying lexical rules in
their discourse production. For example, there
could be rules relating transitive and causative

verbs to morphologically related intransitive and decausative verbs. In English many pairs of this type are morphologically identical (e.g., apply as in "He applied the rule" and apply as in "The rule applies to this example"), while in French it is more common for the intransitive and decausative verbs to be coded with the additional "reflexive" morpheme (e.g., transitive and causative appliquer versus intransitive and decausative s'appliquer. In the abstract approach, errors arise when learners utilize certain facets of the lexical rules in their native language in producing IL forms. It should be noted that this is only a rough sketch of the relevant lexical rules.

The second approach is more concrete. There it is hypothesized that instead of utilizing lexical rules the learner engages in a process of morpheme for morpheme, or word for word, (the question of whether the examples deal with separate words or not is controversial) translation. These two approaches are not equivalent, but there is not enough information to support one over the other.

The IL forms presented are morpheme for morpheme equivalents of the NL verb (here the reflexive is considered part of the verb). In the abstract solution, learners are transferring the facet of the lexical rule relating intransitive/decausative and transitive/causative pairs concerned with the occurrence or omission of an overt reflexive morpheme. In the concrete solution, there is simply a morpheme for morpheme translation. Sentence 4 is more complex because the transitive/causative analogue of marcher is the morphologically unrelated word promener, but the same argument holds.

In the examples presented here, transfer seems to be bidirectional. The forms in Part II suggest that learners treat the prepositions required in verbal complements as "real" prepositions. In an abstract approach, these could be a part of lexical rules. In IL data these putative prepositions are replaced by the translations of the NL prepositions. Again, transfer does seem to be bidirectional. In the IL the same preposition (or lack thereof) is found as in the NL. This is true for both French to English and English to French.

In Part II, the relevant L1 information is the surface representation of constructions. For example, in French, pronouns take many different shapes in different environments (e.g., en, lui, le). French requires that certain prepositions introduce infinitives (e.g., de) while infinitives are not preceded by a preposition in English (with the exception of to). Again, as in Parts I and II, transfer seems to be bidirectional. These data suggest that there is an internal reality to surface morphological facts such as the prepositions required with verbs and in complementizers and the shape of pronouns. That is, the surface facts are salient enough to be transferred into the L2. The influence of lexical subcategorization is seen in the fact that the L1 environments that words are used in influence the environments in which words can be used in the L2.

PROBLEM 2.7

These data come from Dutch learners of English who were asked to judge which examples of breken, break, could be translated into

English. Note that all the sentences given
in the problem are grammatical in Dutch. In
general, when one orders the examples from
most to least translatable, one can see that
those instances of break which are viewed as
possible in the L2 are those which are considered the most usual, the most frequent,
or, as Kellerman (1979) has stated, the
"core" meanings. The reader is referred to
Kellerman's paper for an understanding of
his independent measure of "coreness." One
can hypothesize that the "core" meanings of
a lexical form (see also Problem 4.7) will
be the earliest acquired. With regard to
theories of language transfer, Kellerman,
based on these data, has suggested that
there are aspects of language which are
viewed by the learner as universal and thus
transferable when learning an L2 and other
aspects of language which are viewed as
unique to one's native language and are
thus not transferable to the L2. This can
be seen in the low percentage of translatable responses to those lexical items which
are least core-like. A learner's perception
of language-specific and language-universal
forms changes with increasing proficiency,
and will depend on the L1 and the L2
involved.

    The differences between sentences 3,
6, and 11 are discússed in Kellerman (1983).
The relatively low acceptance of #11 is ex-
plained on the basis of the fact that agent-
less, noncausative break is rejected because
it is considered "marked" vis à vis the
declarative sentence. As Kellerman (1983:121)
states, "Such structures are infrequent,
limited to a few verbs, and display an unusual semantic role for the subject."

PROBLEM 2.8

This problem deals with the acquisition of
word meaning. The data come from 100 native
speakers of Hebrew and 100 learners of Hebrew
as an L2. The results from sentence 1 suggest
that learners tend to select a more general
term iš to cover all the semantic functions
which in Hebrew are covered by other semantically related words. It is also to be noted
that the female counterpart iša, which is
morphologically related to iš, is the only
term used for the various meanings. Sentence
2 shows a similar pattern, although the
tendency is not as strong. Learners are more
or less equally divided between the general
term latet and the specific term lsapeq.
This is in contrast, however, with the NS's
selection of the appropriate (in terms of the
TL) specific lexical item. Thus, lexical
acquisition involves, in part at least, a
"zeroing in" on the specifics of a general
semantic area. This conclusion has its
counterpart in intuitional knowledge. In
Gass (1983) it was shown that learners move
from an overall "feel" for correctness to
a specific analytic understanding of the
forms of an L2.

Sentence 3 does not support the general
conclusion. There are at least two possible
explanations for this. First, it may be a
matter of different stages of acquisition.
That is, it may be that these learners at an
earlier stage did not know the correct form.
They would have selected a more general form.
The other possibility is that the utterance
in question is really a fixed phrase which
may have been learned as a single lexical
item or a fixed collocation.

PROBLEM 3.1

This problem deals with epenthesis. In the Egyptian data in Part I, the learners insert [i] between the first and second consonants of an initial CC cluster. In the Iraqi data, [i] is inserted before the initial cluster.

The data in Part II are native language data illustrating epenthesis in three-consonant clusters. In Egyptian Arabic, the vowel [i] is inserted between the second and third consonants. On the other hand, in the Iraqi Arabic data, [i] is inserted between the first and second consonants.

Learners appear to rely on a NL restriction on the number of consonants allowed in clusters. In the case of Egyptian Arabic, an epenthetic vowel is inserted before the final consonant of a cluster and in Iraqi before a sequence of two consonants. Thus, epenthesis is tied to permissible NL syllable structure.

In Part III, exceptions are given. Given the previous generalizations, the predicted forms are: sitadi, sibasyal, siki. In all cases, we have examples of /s ~ z/ + stop clusters (or /s/ + stop and a rule of voicing assimilation). The explanation for the exceptional behavior of /s/ + stop consonant may be related to a common NL verbal prefix ista which by analogy is extended to all /s/ + stops. On the other hand, one might want to account for these data on the basis of universal principles of sonority. Cross-linguistically, a sonority hierarchy has been postulated such that the following phonological elements can be ordered from least to most

sonorous: stops; fricatives; nasals; liquids;
glides and vowels.   Segments which are
closest to syllable margins tend to be the
least sonorous.   /s/ + stop consonants are
an exception to the hierarchy, and it has
been argued (Selkirk, forthcoming) that in
fact they are treated as a single consonant.
If this is the case, then they are unlikely
to be broken up.   The analysis is supported
by data from languages which do not have the
general epenthesis rules given in this problem.   An·interesting by-product of these
results might be an investigation by students
as to the amount of time which the exceptions,
seen in Part III, persist in the speech of
learners from different NL backgrounds.

<u>PROBLEM 3.2</u>

In Eckman (1981) there is a description of
the experimental tasks involved.   The data
for analysis are pooled.   This can lead to a
discussion of advantages/disadvantages of this
approach to analysis.

The status of underlying forms is controversial in linguistics, not only whether or
not they "exist," but also if they do exist,
what is the nature of these forms?   How one
justifies underlying form for IL's can be
raised as part of class discussion.

There are cases in these data where
there are alternations: for example, [p-b];
[t-ð]; [k-g]; [f-v]; [t-d] and cases where
there are not (for example, /wet-wetter/).
The individuals differ as can be seen in
[f-v] (<u>brave-braver</u>) for subject 1 and [v],
no alternation, (<u>rob-robber</u>) for subject 2.

For subject 1, fricatives are voiceless
in word final positions. In intervocalic
position, there is a general tendency for
there to be voiced obstruents. There are
examples of intervocalic fricatives alter-
nating with intervocalic stops, but there are
also examples where this alternation does
not occur (wet-wetter). However, it is in
just those examples in which "underlyingly"
there are voiced consonants where spirantization occurs (exception is Bob-Bobby).
There is also a possibility of morphophonemic
alternations (-est suffixes do not condition
spirantization), although there are too few
examples to know this for sure.

For subject 2, there are examples of
alternations (Bob-Bobby) as well as no
alternations (rob-robber). There are no
examples of this latter type for speaker 1.
There are numerous examples of intervocalic
spirantization, although, as with speaker
1, there are also examples where this
alternation is not apparent. Both speakers
deviate from TL norms by producing voiceless
forms where the TL produces voiced forms,
but not the reverse. With one exception
(fuzzy), these deviations occur in word-
final position. Similarly, errors in
spirantization are in the same direction
for both speakers. Spirants occur where
stops do in standard English, but one does
not find the reverse.

To provide variable rule descriptions,
one would want to describe the environments
in which a particular TL variant is found
(e.g., [t → ð/front vowel; t→d/back vowel;
t→t/underlying /t/) and the percentage of
each.

To posit underlying forms in IL's, one must assume that the learner has some knowledge of what s/he is aiming for and that there is then a rule which takes him/her from the targeted form to the produced form. An underlying form of /wet/ vs. /red/ nicely accounts for the difference between the comparative forms of these two words for both subjects. The difficulty in positing underlying forms is selecting the appropriate form. Because learners notice that there is a difference between two forms does not necessarily mean that they perceive the same difference that native speakers do. It is quite possible that what is salient for the NNS's (in this case probably native speakers as well) is the difference in vowel length and not the consonant difference. Thus, attributing a difference in underlying forms to the consonant may be misleading. On the other hand, not positing underlying forms may preclude any explanations and ignores the fact that some patterning exists.

PROBLEM 3.3

The data in this problem come from the same study as those in Problem 3.2. These data are from two Mandarin speakers. Both speakers have examples of word final voiced obstruents apparently in free variation with word final / ə / following voiced obstruents. This differs from the IL phonetics of the two Spanish speakers presented in Problem 3.2. These two are much more similar in their phonetics than were the Spanish speakers. The following underlying forms were posited in Eckman (1981).

The same arguments presented in Problem 3.2
for and against the use of underlying forms in
IL are relevant here.

Subject	IL underlying form	Gloss
1	/tæg/	tag
	/rab/	rob
	/hæd/	had
	/hiz/	he's
	/smuðə/	smoother
	/rayt/	right
	/dɛk/	deck
	/zɪp/	zip
	/mɪs/	mis
	/wɛt/	wet
	/dɪfər/	differ
	/ovər/	over
	/bɪgər/	bigger
	/kɪkɪn/	kicking
	/tæpɪn/	tapping
	/lebər/	label
	/lɛər/	letter
	/blidɪn/	bleeding
	/lidə/	leader
2	/ænd/	and
	/hæd/	had
	/tɔb/	tub
	/stadɾd/	started
	/fɪU d/	filled
	/bɪg/	big
	/rɛkənayzd/	recognized
	/ɪz/	is
	/sɛz/	says
	/wɔtə/	water
	/afə/	offer
	/lidə/	leader

PROBLEM 3.4

The topic of this problem is the variable pronunciation of the TL /r/ by Japanese students. What is noteworthy is the fact that the pronunciation is variable. The bar graphs in Part II suggest that the variability is phonetically conditioned. While more than one variant is selected in a particular environment, the following vowel is important in determining whether the variant selected is TL-like or not and, if not, which of the non-TL variants is selected. Vowel height then determines both the selection and the frequency of the variants.

In Part III are graphed the results of the accuracy of use of the NL variant /r/ in two phonetic environments and three speech styles. The TL pronunciation is, in general, more accurate preceding mid-vowels than high vowels (as was also seen in Part II). In addition, within each phonetic environment, there is an ordering of styles from least accurate in free speech to most accurate in the reading of a word list. In fact, the accuracy rate is higher preceding a high vowel on the word list task than preceding a mid-vowel on the free speech task. In general, there is systematicity in the Japanese pronunciation of English /r/. The IL variants are determined by speech style as well as by phonetic environment.

PROBLEM 3.5

	Final Consonants		Consonant Clusters	
	Deletion	Epenthesis	Deletion	Epenthesis
Korean #1	10 (59%)	4 (24%)	2 (12%)	1 (5%)
Korean #2	10 (67%)	3 (20%)	2 (13%)	0
Canton-ese #1	10 (40%)	8 (32%)	7 (28%)	0
Canton-ese #2	13 (45%)	11 (38%)	5 (17%)	0
Portu-guese #1	2 (11%)	11 (58%)	2 (11%)	4 (20%)
Portu-guese #2	0	8 (80%)	2 (20%)	0

	# Errors	# Errors due to language transfer	Non-transfer errors
Korean #1	17	9 (53%)	8 (47%)
Korean #2	15	11 (73%)	4 (27%)
Canton-ese #1	25	19 (77%)	6 (23%)
Canton-ese #2	29	21 (73%)	8 (27%)
Portu-guese #1	19	16 (84%)	3 (16%)
Portu-guese #2	10	9 (90%)	1 (10%)

Most syllable structure errors were due to NL transfer. For those instances which cannot be accounted for on the basis of NL transfer, one can postulate that there is an attempt to "simplify" the L2 syllable structure to a basic CV pattern (cf. Clements and Keyser 1983 for an argument of a CV syllable structure as the universally basic syllable structure). Thus learners tend to modify their syllable structure so that the resultant IL form is a universally preferred open syllable (usually CV). As a follow-up, students might want to compare the IL speech of learners whose NL has open syllables as opposed to those without.

PROBLEM 3.6

Among the phonological processes are:

1. deletions

kvartira	xabartir-
vstreča	-streča
molodoj	mol-doj
bolezn'	boles'-
vtoraja	-taraja
vstaval	-staval

2. insertions

kvatira	xabartir
čort	šorta
priznal	piriznal
brigadir	birgardir

3. metathesis

afrika	aperxa
rabočij	arbočij
krugom	kurgom

4. consonant weakening (stop fricative; affricate fricative)

kvartira	x̱abartira
čort	š̌orta

5. changes in vowel quality

afrika	aperx̱a
krugom	kür̄gøm

[Note that the o̱ in vtoraja is pronounced as [a] in stan̄dard Russian and many dialects.]

In general, the interlanguage forms have simpler syllable structure than those of Russian, but it is difficult, if not impossible, to predict exactly which process will be selected to yield the IL form. For example, for priznal a vowel is inserted, for vstaval a consonant is deleted, but for krugom the consonant and vowel are metathesized. The most basic fact is that the IL forms approximate the TL forms, but the nature of the approximation varies. Furthermore, when Russian consonants change, they either weaken or delete.

PROBLEM 3.7

For initial R, a difference can be seen dependent on the data source. In the data stemming from free conversation, there is a larger percentage of TL-based forms; whereas in the data based on the reading of word lists, there is a much larger percentage of NL-based elements. Two relevant notions are: 1) permeability (Adjemian 1976); and 2) style-shifting in terms of amount of attention paid to speech (Tarone 1979; 1982). For final R, the issue is more problematic since Thai has no final R. Here again one sees differences

dependent on the data source. However, the
results point in the opposite direction. There
are more TL variants in the listing data and
more NL-based variants in the conversational
data. One could argue that the / ∅ / and / ə /
are, in fact, correct TL variants since these
forms are the TL variants these learners are
often exposed to. This raises the important
point of the relationship between input, exposure, and IL grammars. When exposed to poten-
tially contradictory data, how do learners
select one variety over another? (Cf. Beebe,
1985, for a review of some relevant issues.)

The data in Part II should be amended with
the heading "Initial R" replaced by the heading
"Interference" followed by "Initial R." The
table should thus be:

Percentage of error due to interference
and creation of new IL variants for R variable

Cause of error	Speech style	
	Conversation	Listing
Initial R		
Interference [ř], [r̃], [l̥]	6.2	39.4
New Variants [ɹ́], [wɹ́], [ɹ̥], [ɹ̥], [ɾ̥], [ɪ̯]	93.8	60.6
Final R		

Thus, the three phonetic variants [ř], [r̃],
[ḷ] are NL variants. NL variants have little
effect on the IL here, most variants being
newly created ones. Importantly, the results
differ depending on the type of elicitation
measure used. Transfer occurs in the more
formal context in which there is greater
attention paid to speech. This follows the
well-attested fact that IL data from the same
learner varies with the task used to elicit
the data. Discussion can proceed on the
question of why this should be so and its
effect on IL descriptions.

The data in Part III show that phonetic
transfer is at times dependent on sociolinguistic factors as well as purely linguistic
ones. The NL formal variant [r̃] is used
most frequently in the formal task and is
not used at all in free conversation.

PROBLEM 4.1

These data are from the same learners as
presented in Problems 1.2; 1.7; and 2.3. The
concern in this problem is with number agreement. In general, there seems to be little
evidence of the use of agreement in these
data. For a more detailed analysis, we rec-
ommend dividing the data in Part I into
three groups: 1) 1-6; 2) 7-8; and 3) 9.
In sentences 1-6, the learners appear to be
choosing the English "simple form" of the
verb for the singular subject in each case.
This, of course, differs from standard
English usage which, in most cases, adds an
-s to the verb stem. For singular subjects,
sentences 7-8 provide the use of a possible

"unanalyzed unit" for the existential <u>there is/
there are</u>. Interestingly, NS's of English
often do the same thing, but with one important exception — NS's use the contracted and
not the full form. Sentence 9 provides an
example of a complex sentence where <u>vocabulary</u>
is clearly pluralized, <u>many vocabulary</u>, as a
count noun, whereas the pronoun referring to
it is the singular <u>it</u>. A question arises as
to whether <u>it means</u> is a formulaic expression
or not.

The data in Part II complicate the
analysis and suggest the important lesson of
not generalizing too quickly. The learners
could have two "coexistent" IL systems here,
one TL-like and one not (see Selinker 1984).
An argument based on two separate systems is
a difficult one to make. One would want to
know the conditions under which the two forms
are used. One possibility is that sentences
from an earlier stage may be produced under
some conditions. Only a longitudinal study
that has relevant prior data from these
learners could settle this question. Additional data from these learners could provide
information about the context of forms.

PROBLEM 4.2

In sentences 6 and 7 the assumed subject
is <u>we</u>. In all instances these learners appear
to have hypothesized that infinitive modifiers
come last in a sentence. Possible TL interpretations for the sentences are as follows
(see Corder 1981 for a discussion of problems
of interpreting IL sentences):

1. There are some people who get
   married several times.
2. While I was walking down the
   street, I found a poster which
   was advertising the coming
   dance concert.
3. There are some differences
   which represent the national
   character.
4. I've planned to have a farewell
   party for a friend who is going
   to the mainland.
5. There are many boys in Japan
   who like baseball.
6. In a cafeteria we will take the
   dish we want to eat.
7. We can go to places we want to
   go to faster by using a car.

Infinitive modifiers are used in the IL
where the TL uses relative clause modification.
The subject is adjacent to the modifier in just
those instances when it is a matter of subject
relativization (1-5) and it is not adjacent
when it is not subject relativization. This
could be tested by grammaticality judgments
and instances of other types of relative
clauses (such as indirect object, object of
comparative, etc.).

PROBLEM 4.3

A possible explanation for the use and lack
of use of articles has to do with numbers of
modifiers. The article is not used in instances where there is another noun modifier.
For example, from sea castle, in small village,
of sea castle, by beautiful girls, to true world

versus <u>the turtle</u>, <u>one turtle in the sea</u>.
There are apparent exceptions: <u>on the seaside</u>,
<u>the new world</u>, and <u>in Japan</u>. Upon closer con-
sideration, however, they may not be counter-
examples at all. In <u>on the seaside</u>, <u>seaside</u> is
written as one word, suggesting that this was
not an example of word combination. Rather,
<u>seaside</u> is a single lexical item for this
learner, unlike <u>sea castle</u>. Japanese speakers
have informed us that <u>new world</u> is a very frequently used combination and as such is considered to be a unit. Hence, again there is not
active word combination. The final apparent
counter-example is <u>in Japan</u>. If the rule of
article usage with unmodified nouns is correct,
then one would expect <u>in the Japan</u>. However,
the lack of article in this instance can be
accounted for by actual knowledge of English
with regard to place names. Class discussion
can center around the reasonableness of these
explanations.

It is to be noted that many of the uses of
<u>a</u> are within fixed phrases (<u>once upon a time</u>,
<u>get a chance</u>, <u>take a walk</u>), or sentence frames
(<u>there is a</u>). How one conceives of and deals
with such examples is a matter of theoretical
import since productive use of a rule is quite
different from using fixed phrases. One could
test the accuracy of the generalizations suggested here through an examination of more
compositions or through elicitation procedures
aimed at forcing learners to make a <u>choice</u>
regarding the relevant structures (Corder 1981).

The data from the second composition show
an almost total absence of articles. The exception is in line 8, where this learner uses <u>a</u>
<u>possibility</u> and <u>a problem</u>. These may be part
of learned sentence frames (see Problem 4.6):

<u>that's a</u> X and <u>there is a</u> X. This learner,
like the one who wrote composition 1, does not
use articles in prepositional phrases. The
difference is that the first learner did use
articles in prepositional phrases when there
was no other modification.

PROBLEM 4.4

These data come from a longitudinal study
of a Japanese child's acquisition of English.
At Time 1 she forms questions using the simple
present. At Time 2 she begins to form questions
using the progressive. <u>What do you</u> appears at
the beginning of each question in the IL. It
appears that <u>do you</u> is a prefabricated unit in
Hakuta's (1974) terms, in this case used as a
question marker. In other words, it is treated
as a single lexical unit. <u>What</u> and <u>how</u> further
specify the type of question. Evidence for <u>do</u>
<u>you</u> as an unanalyzed unit comes from the seeming
tags at the end of sentences at Time 2. The
tags are the semantic subjects of the question.
Thus, <u>what do you doing, this boy</u> is to
be interpreted as "What is this boy doing?"
One can reasonably hypothesize that the forms
at Time 1 are deceivingly correct. That is,
the <u>do you</u> form coincides with English usage in
those instances even though the learner's analysis is not the same as that of a native
English speaker.

In Part II the child begins in Month 3 with
verbs in the present tense + <u>do you</u>. In Months
4 and 5 there is evidence of reanalysis of the
<u>do you</u> form since she now produces both <u>did you</u>
and <u>do you</u>. During Months 6 through 8 there
are alternative forms for past tense questions.
Either the main verb is inflected (e.g.,

bought — put is unclear) or the auxiliary do is
inflected or, as in Month 8, both are used
"did everybody saw some blue hairs?" By Month
9 she appears to have sorted out the relevant
information for past tense questions in English.

There are at least two pieces of evidence
to bring to bear on the issue of gradual acquisition. First, she moves from a) constructions
which are limited but correct to b) constructions which are in large part incorrect to
c) those which are in large part correct. Even
at this point, however, there are a number of
incorrect forms from a TL point of view. In
this sense, we would claim gradual acquisition.
A second way of viewing the notion of gradual-
ness is to consider the Wh- forms used at a
given time. For example, there are a number of
instances of what questions during Months 5 and
6. These are only in the past tense (see Month
4 for an exception). Why questions do not
appear until four months later — at Time 10.
Thus, if we consider pooled different Wh- words,
acquisition is gradual. On the other hand, if
we consider each Wh- word separately, there is
evidence to claim that it is abrupt, since they
appear to focus on one Wh- word at a time until
they have "learned" it. Types of evidence to
disentangle these alternative claims could be
the focus of useful class discussion.

PROBLEM 4.5

According to the data in Part I, these
learners form questions in English by using
affirmative sentences along with (most likely)
rising intonation, as is done in most of the
world's languages. Considering the data from a
TL point of view, these learners do not use do.

Interestingly, #3, #4, and #5 are possible
questions in English, but are semantically or
pragmatically "marked."   In gathering L2 data
of this type, it would be interesting to
determine the IL function of these questions,
perhaps through NL-playback techniques.
Questions 1 and 2 are interesting because the
learners may have generalized question formation to the embedded environment.   Another
possibility is that these learners are sensitive
to the informal spoken environment of standard
English in which these forms are common.

In Part II, with the exception of #2 in
which do is used, these students appear to have
developed the IL pattern for Wh- questions of
using the affirmative sentence order with the
Wh- word placed initially.   This is clearly the
expected pattern given the data of Part I.

In Part III we present questions with do,
arriving at a similar analysis as in Part II.
In all of these sentences the learners may have
come up with an IL generalization such as the
following: add a question word (do or did) to
affirmative word order.   The concept of
inversion would be superfluous with this analysis.   Thus, the IL result would be identical
to the TL result, yet the analysis underlying
each would differ.   It is important to keep in
mind that we do not know the IL function of
these questions and that "covert errors"
(Corder 1981) are always possible (see also
Problem 4.4).   Sentence 10 is interesting in
this regard since it shows the possibility of
overgeneralizing do questions to environments
(in this case, questions with be) not appropriate in the TL.   This brings up a related
point: just because one has congruence in the
IL to expected TL-norms (sentences 1 through 9)

does not necessarily mean that learners have mastered the TL requisite form/function correspondence. This is a point which IL analysis should always bear in mind.

PROBLEM 4.6

These data are from a longitudinal study of several Mexican-American children living in California. If one assumes that lookit, looky, and look are variants of some sort of pointing marker (the function), then one could hypothesize the following pattern, or sentence frame:

[X] [open class of those pointed to]

where X = lookit, looky, or look. (Note that it is unclear which one of the three is chosen and why.) Wong-Fillmore (1976:294 - 95) states that "sentence formula" are needed "to refer to language which functioned wholly or partly as unanalyzed, fixed, or automatic units for the speaker." She further states that in her study, units which are formulaic refer to "fluid, evolving systems of expressions." Thus, there are two points here: units that are unanalyzed and such units evolving over time.

The VP IL units in Part II (1,2,5,6), which function as a sentence frame or formula, appear to be:

Is [-verb form] [-open N class]

Precisely why the verb in one case is -ing and in another got is unclear. Concerning the function of it (note that #3 has no it), one might have, as in Part I, a pointing marker, as

we saw in Part I with <u>looky</u>, <u>lookit</u>, <u>look</u>.
Sentence 4 provides support for this interpretation. Another possible interpretation is
that it may have a syntactic function, a place
holder. The data in the Appendix should
strengthen the notion of sentence formula or
frame. It appears to be common in IL's that
such formulae play a crucial role in L2 acquisition, perhaps as "social strategies" as
Wong-Fillmore suggests. Such formulae are
clearly candidates for fossilization by some
learners, but not all; other learners go on to
analyze them. An interesting class discussion
could be geared toward why this may be the case
for some learners, but not all.

PROBLEM 4.7

For the progressive:

9 > 2 > 6 > 3 & 4

For the simple present:

14 > 5 > 1 > 11 > 7

For the future:

8 > 10 > 12 & 13

Perhaps the most striking feature is the
low acceptability of sentences describing states
or events whose time frame is not associated
with the core (basic) meaning, i.e., 1) future
states or events for the future; 2) present
states or events for the progressive or simple
present. This suggests that the acquisition
of some aspects of syntax is dependent on the

semantic function of syntactic structures.   In
considering sentences 4 and 7, we see that
Spanish speakers are not simply translating
from Spanish and transferring the Spanish acceptability judgments for the English-based
task.   Rather, they appear to be basing their
judgments on the core meanings of these items
(which are universally determined).

For Part II, we note the following ranks:
9 > 4 > 6 > 2 > 3 (progressive); 14 > 5 > 11 >
1 > 7 (simple present); and 10 > 8 > 12 > 13
(future).   It is to be noted that some differences (e.g., 1 and 11) are so minor that they
may be accidental.   The only sentences which
come in radically different positions in the
hierarchy are 2 (second in Spanish, fourth in
Japanese) and 4 (tied for fourth and fifth in
Spanish, second in Japanese).   Sentence 4 is
said to be possible in Spanish, but it is not
within the core meaning range.   It is possible
that the Spanish speakers rejected 4 since it
was felt to be too Spanish-particular.   Sentence 2 concerns the progressive usage of see.
See only rarely occurs within the progressive
(I see the tree vs. I am looking at the tree).
This unusualness of progressive see may be the
reason for the low acceptability for this sentence by Japanese learners.   The restrictions
on the use of progressive see are virtually the
same in Spanish as in English.   Possibly they,
through their knowledge of Spanish, recognized
this as an unusual situation in which progressive see is possible.   Possibly, as with 4, they
considered the lexical restriction against progressive see as too Spanish-particular and thus
assumed it could not be freely used in English.
In general, one can say that the specific differences in percentages between the two groups
may be determined by language-specific distances

on the continuum from core to peripheral
meanings. General rankings may be due
to universal facts. Acquisition
clearly seems to be gradual, since not
all forms are used appropriately at the
same time.

PROBLEM 4.8

These data come from a conversation with
a NS of English learning Spanish in Puerto
Rico. The data were organized by
Andersen (1983, Table 2) in such a way so
that all utterances which result in
"no violation" in Spanish SVO order are
listed in the left column, whereas those
with a preverbal clitic pronoun are listed
in the right column. See pages 48 to 51. He
states that it could be argued that these sentences are evidence of a strategy that produces
SVO order (or SV where there is no object).
Gustar "to please" which takes an IO can be
contrasted to the English semantic equivalent
"to like," which takes a DO. Within a Contrastive Analysis framework, the subject and object
are reversed in Spanish and English. Thus, the
IL sentences in (12) could be interpreted as
evidence for lexical transfer in that the
learner appears to interpret gustar as identical in meaning and function to like (see also
Dvorak 1983 and Dvorak and Kirshner 1982).

The five utterances in (7), however, show correct placement of clitic pronouns with gustar, though there are other minor errors as well. Andersen points to the sentence in (5) which contains a noun (cosas) which should have been a pronoun (las). This suggests the possibility that the learner does not know the correct form or placement of the pronoun, and displays an avoidance strategy.

Turning to the three utterances in (4), Andersen has them listed as *(se), *(se), *(me), which indicates that in Spanish these are reflexive sentences, but not so in English. By failing to supply the reflexive pronoun, the learner could be following English rather than Spanish.

If students have access to Andersen's article, they can be referred to Table 8 in which Andersen shows 100% accuracy with preverbal reflexive pronouns. Thus, there does seem to be some productive control of this grammatical area.

One can only show consistent word order if one were to follow through with some principled contextual application of word order. Andersen speculates on his subject being between an "earlier stage" with variable word order and a later more TL-like stage.

TABLE

LEFT COLUMN

Number in Workbook	SVO order
11	1.
6	2. *(me) *(lo) *(lo) *(la)
12	3. *(le) *(me) *(le)
5	4. *(las)
4	5. *(se) *(se) *(me)
13	6. *(las) *(los)
2	7. *

LEFT COLUMN (continued)

SVO order (continued)

	V	O
...con otro amigo	ayudándome	
Y (ellos) no puedo	hacerlo	pa...
...ahi adentro	ayudándolo	
...si puedamo	cogerlo	bien.
...no está listo pa	casarse.	
Ello va a	llamar	a mi pa 'cer...
...que sa fue pa	buscar	él.
Pero yo no Ø	vi	él mucho.
Yo sólo Ø	visité	la dos veces.
Ø El no Ø	gustaba	los americanos.
Yo Ø	gusta	todo...
Ø El no Ø	gusta	mucho problema.
...así pa xxx	vender*	cosas.
...pregunta a	casar	Ø con ella.
Y ella tenía que	quedar	Ø en el lobby.
Pue yo Ø	quedo	con él.
pue Ø	ponemo	en cajas...
Ello(s) Ø	usaba	pa el companía.
...si la mamá no lo	dejó	Raymond salir...

TABLE (continued)

RIGHT COLUMN

Number in Workbook	SOV order
9	8.
7	9.
1	10.
10	11.
8	12.
3	13.

RIGHT COLUMN (continued)

SOV order (continued)

	O	V
Y la, ell(as)	sa	fueron.
Pue, todo	sa	fue.((=se fueron))
Ella	sa	fue.
...que	sa	fue pa buscar él.
Ella	sa	fue solo a S.F....
*Yo creo que yo	me	gusta menos.
No	me	gusta ni...
No	me	gustaba.
* ∅ El no	le	gustaba mucho,...
Ella...que no	me	gustaba ella.
Depué cuando	nos	aguantamos por el manos.
Pero porque	me	mudó aquí...(=mudé)
Yo no	me	acuerdo.
Ya no	me	acuerdo.
Yo no	me	acuerdo del otro.
No	me	acuerdo.
El maestro que	me	ensañaba espanõl...
...él	me	contesta en inglés.
Pue él, ello	me	cambió...
No, ello todavia	me	llamaron.
Cuando	me	llaman.
A ver si	me	llaman pa pelota.

*(∅) O caminá-,o	*me	camino o en bicicleta.
*(∅)	*Se	vivia en Palmas.
*(se)	*esquedar y	esquedar.(=se quedaba y se quedaba)

PROBLEM 4.9

These data were gathered from Israeli students learning English. The data come from interview situations.

The slash in each sentence in the data in Part I is intended to make it easier for students to focus on a certain phenomenon: in this case, strings of linguistic material which appear after the verb. Before dealing with possible IL generalizations to account for the order of elements, one must first postulate what the elements or units are. The units in the post verbal material are: object [OB], time [TI], place [PL], and adverb [ADV] strings, set up as follows.

1.	OB-TI	12.	OB-TI
2.	OB-TI	13.	TI-PL
3.	OB-PL	14.	TI-PL
4.	PL-OB	15.	TI-PL
5.	OB-ADV	16.	TI-PL
6.	ADV-OB	17.	PL-TI
7.	PL-TI	18.	PL-TI
8.	TI-PL	19.	ADV-OB
9.	OB-PL	20.	OB-TI
10.	OB-PL	21.	OB-PL
11.	PL-OB		

These orderings are called "two-choice schemas" (Selinker 1969, reprinted in Gass and Selinker 1983), i.e., one gets either [a-b] or [b-a] orderings; there are no other choices.

If OB is divided into N + ProN, the following IL generalization holds: whenever there are two strings after the verb in this IL, if one is a pronoun, it will occur first. Another generalization that holds is that: whenever

there are two strings after the verb, if one is
OB and the other is TI, the order will be OB-TI.
Concerning the other combinations of strings,
we have seemingly random order:

> OB-PL 3,9,10,21
>
> PL-OB 4,11 — where OB is a noun
>
> TI-PL 8,13,14,15,16
>
> PL-TI 17,18
>
> OB-ADV 5
>
> ADV-OB 6,19

More data might possibly reveal tendencies, for
example in OB-PL data there is a tendency for
the OB element to come first. Similarly, for
TI-PL, there is a tendency for TI to come
first. One could generalize even further that
the place element appears second after the
verb.

  The data in Part II do and do not complicate the analysis set up in Part I.

  Sentence 1: does not complicate it
      because there is only one string
      after the verb

  Sentence 2: shows that a TI string can
      occur preverbally. This compli-
      cates the analysis if this position
      is restricted to only certain of
      the strings concerned.

  Sentences 3 and 4: show that PL strings
      can occur postverbally in their IL.
      The statistics for a three-choice
      schema [a-b-c] are much more

complex than for the two-choice
schema [a-b] we have postulated
for the data in Part I.

Sentences 5 and 6: these are like
sentence 2 with a PL and ADV
string, respectively

Sentences 7-11: like sentence 2

Sentence 13: presents a new unit
for a present and follows the
IL rule of pronoun OB first

Sentences 14 and 16: like sentence 1

Sentence 15:   pronoun OB + TI string

Sentence 17: this is complex and in TL
terms lacks a verb to be. The
reinterpretation in TL terms being
The Israeli singer I like best is
Rivka Michael. The complexity
lies in the occurrence in the
sentence of a reduced restrictive
clause (whom) I like best.

Sentence 18: like sentence 6

Sentences 19 and 20: like sentence 2

With regard to Part III, about half of the
sentences follow the bias of having the question appear to affect the response:

A. no
   yes
   yes
   no
   yes
   yes
   yes

B. yes for all

C. yes
   no
   no
   yes
   no
   yes
   no

D. yes
   no
   no
   no
   no
   no

E. yes for all

Concerning question 5, an analysis of the fuller data set should help to solve some of the questions raised above. Complete statistics for the full data set are given in Selinker (1969). This can be resolved by returning to the original data and counting. Additionally, another bit of relevant evidence would involve parallel TL data gathered from NS's of the TL. For example, <u>not once</u> in the data with NS's, after a question of the type "What singer do you like <u>best</u>?" does one get an answer of the type "I <u>like best X.</u>" Andersen (1983) argues strongly that parallel NS data should regularly be gathered.

Reflecting on question 4 should lead to a discussion of "how much is enough data?" and to the conclusion that the answer is arbitrary, i.e., any experiment is still a pilot study. Another question often discussed in this regard is that without clear hypotheses to test, one might "drown" in data.

PROBLEM 5.1

Continuing the format set up in the
Workbook, the data can be categorized as
follows:

Past   Present

... and noisy outside
the house or outside
the apartment and he
woke up in a bad tem-
per and he wanted a
fresh air, he went
when he opened the
window to get this
fresh air, he found
a smoke, smoke air,
dirty air. The movie
also showed that the
man not only disturbed
in his special apart-
ment or special house,
but in everything, in
work, in street, in
transportation, even
in the gardens and
seashores.

Man in the city has to
wake up very early to go
to the work and he has
to as the movie shows,
he has to use any means
of transportation, car,
bus, bicycle, and all
the streets are crowded,
and he has no no choice
or alternatively to use
and he is busy day and
night. At day he has to

Past	Present
	work hard among the machines, among the typewriters and among papers, pencils and offices in the city. And when
he wanted to take a rest in his house or outside his house in the garden or the sea-shore ...	
	He can't because the streets are crowded with people.
When he wanted to take a meal in restaurant,	
	the restaurant is crowd-ed, everything is crowded in the city and very, very - it's not good place or good atmos-phere to to live in ...
the movie showed that. And the man began to feel sick and thus he wanted to consult the doctors to describe a medicine or anything for-for health, but the doctors also disagreed about his illness or they couldn't diagnose his illness correctly.	
	this they show at first. Want to make us know about the life in the city.
The man began to think about to find a solution	

Past

Present

or answer for this
dilemma. OK dil-
emma? Dilemma. He
thought that why not
to go to the open
lands and to build
houses and gardens and
live in this new fresh
land with fresh air
and fresh atmosphere
and

Why don't we stop smoking
in the factories by using
filters, filters and stop
smoking from the cars and
all industrial bad sur-
vivals or like smoking
like dirty airs and so
on.

The man also wanted to
make kids or childrens
in the houses not to
play or to use sports
inside houses, but to
go outside the houses
in the garden and to
play with balls, basket,
anything

they like to play.

And also he wanted to
live in a quiet and
calm apartment.

People inside houses must
not use T.V. in a bad way
or a noisy way. Must use
it in a calm way or in
a quiet way and that, I
think, that is a good
solution or a good

Past	Present
	answer for this city dilemma.

In this retelling of a movie, tense shifts
are used primarily in two ways although they
are not independent of one another. First,
tense shifts coincide with topic shifts and
second, they are used to move from specific
statements about the movie (e.g., The movie
began ... (past)) to generic statements about
life in the city. (Man in the city has to wake
up ... (present)). These generic statements
go beyond a retelling of the events of the
movie to include the message, or moral, of the
movie. Included in these are often evaluative
statements, as can be seen in the last line of
the report. Clearly, these two functions are
interrelated since switching from specific to
generic statements involves a topic shift.

One also notes other grammatical devices
involved in conjunction with tense shifts. In
the past the word man is always preceded by an
article (a man, the man). In the present, there
is only one instance of the word man. It is
not preceded by an article, thus, emphasizing
the generic message the NNS attempts to get
across.

Below is the categorization into past versus
present for the written version of the same
text.

Past	Present
I saw a movie about a man in a city (big city)	
	I want to tell you
what I saw	

Past	Present
	and what is my opinion
The movie began with a man forty years old, in his apartment in a big city. He was disturbed by many things like Alarm O'Clock, T.V., Radio and noisy outside.	
	He want a fresh air,
but he could not because	
	the city is not a good place for fresh air. There are many factories which fill the air with smoke.
The movie showed the daily life of a man in the city.	
	He is very busy day and night.
he had to go to his work early by any means of transportation, car, bus, bicycle.	
	The streets are crowded, everything in the city is crowded with people, the houses, streets, factories, institutions and even the seashores. Man in a big city lives a hard and unhealthy life, noisy, dirt air, crowded houses and smoke are good factors for sickness.
The man in the big city tried to find an answer	

Past	Present
to this dilemma. Instead of living in crowded, unhealthy and big city, he wanted places that	
	must be used for living. People must live in good atmosphere climate and land. Gardens, which are good places for sports, must surround houses. My opinion is that man's solution for the problem is good and acceptable especially for health.

The function of the tense shifts is similar.
However, what is interesting and perhaps unexpected is the fact that there are proportionately more tense shifts in the written as opposed to the spoken version. The NNS shifts tenses 15 times in the spoken version and 13 times in the written version data yet the former contains approximately twice as much language data as the latter. It appears that in general this is the case because the NNS elaborates more in the spoken version. That is, the tense shifts occur in similar places; it is the amount of information given after each instance of tense shift which differs.

The beginning of the written version is particularly revealing for pointing out the shift from specific to generic statements. The writer begins by setting the scene in the past I saw a movie, then he immediately switches to the present tense to draw the reader into his retelling by writing I want to

tell you. This is followed by a switch in the
embedded clause that follows to the past tense
to again refer specifically to the movie what
I saw. Again, there is an immediate tense
shift to the present and what is my opinion
to set the scene for the evaluative comments
that he will make. Next, begins the telling of
the movie in the past The movie began ....

As in the spoken version, there is an
interesting use and lack of use of articles in
this essay, corresponding with specific and
generic themes. There are six instances of the
use of the word man, four in a past context,
two in a present context. Those in a past
context are preceded by either a or the and
those in the present context which have a more
generic meaning are not preceded by an article.

PROBLEM 5.2

The data from this problem come from an
Italian speaker who performs the same task as
the Arabic speaker in Problem 5.1.

Following the format of Problem 5.1, the
data can be categorized as follows:

Past   Present

So it there was a movie,
um probably filmed* some
years ago in
Budapest ... from ... it
was a Hungarian film? a
Hungarian film. It was
a cartoon, and it dealt
with modern life in the
big city. The man who
uh well the

Past	Present
	It is a description of the life of a man in a big city. From morning when he wakes up and go to work with many other people all living in the same ... under the same circumstances and uh with the same patern- istic form in the big city. And from a very common description of life of modern life, of our pressure, of our stress, of our anxie- ties and of all the um possible uh limits and uh rules we have to follow living in a big city. And it deals also with uh
it dealt with pollution problems in a town, in a city where industry and uh residential areas are very close together.	
	And ... the moral of the story is uh that if people could* do some- thing all together the population would have the courage and the will to do eh something for ... to deal with those problems that may reasonably be able to find a solution or to encourage authorities to face the problem ...

Past   Present
                                  and to find solutions
                                  to the ... to it,
                                  because it's not so
                                  difficult in fact.

---

*It is not clear how one wants to categorize
these vis à vis the present/past distinction.

This NNS focusses much of his description,
not on the facts of the movie, but on the
meaning behind the movie. There seem to be two
main purposes for using the past: 1) to set
the scene, and 2) to summarize. He begins in
the past by giving background information about
the movie (where it was filmed, type of movie,
and the message). The only other use of the
past comes as he is giving a summary of the
specifics of the film (it dealt with pollution
problems ...). Note that this follows a "false
start" in which the NNS begins in the present
and it deals also. The referent of it in it
deals is most likely the generic message of
the film, whereas the NNS switches to it dealt
and focussed on a summary of the film. Unlike
the data in Problem 5.1, the present/past distinction does not correspond to a specific/
generic distinction. Both are included in the
use of the present tense by this NNS. Another
use of the present for this speaker is to
express the moral of the story and ... the
moral of the story is ....

One could also claim that in fact there is
little productive use of the past in the story.
All examples of past tense can be considered
part of a storytelling formula: there was a,
it was a, it dealt with. Further evidence of
this comes from the false start in line 7 in

which the speaker is telling the story in the
present and then makes a switch to the past,
using a storytelling formula.   This raises
the important question of sentence frames and
language use in specific domains (cf. Selinker
and Douglas, in press).

Past   Present

The film dealt mainly
with problems concern-
ing our modern life in
a big city.

                              The main character of
                              the story is ... (the
                              rest is in the present)

    The tense shifting in the written version
is minimal. He begins by setting the scene, a
summary of the movie, in the past. This is
similar to the use of the past in the spoken
version. The rest of the description is in the
present and deals with specifics of the movie
(the film describes his everyday life and shows
him in ...) and general statements transcending
the events of the movie (the author of the
story tell us about general and very common
problems of a modern city ...).

    Comparing these descriptions with those of
the Arabic speaker, we find that in both cases
tense shifting is associated with a topic shift.
In the first case, the topic shift corresponds
to a difference in the general/specific domain
and in the second the past is used for statements which can be considered as either setting
the scene or providing a summary (both of which
are in a sense providing background information),
whereas the present is used for both specific
and generic statements.

An interesting difference is the focus of
the description. In addition to dealing with
the message of the film, the NNS in Problem
5.1 gives a fair amount of detail about the
specific facts of the film (The man is disturbed by an alarm clock, radio, T.V., etc.).
These latter facts are absent from the NNS's
description of Problem 5.2. He concentrates
on the specifics only in general terms and
focusses his attention on the message. This
difference is perhaps reflected in the instances of the word man (the subject of the
film) which each speaker uses. The first NNS
uses the word (both in its specific and generic
sense) seven times in the spoken version and
six in the written version, whereas the second
NNS used it twice in the spoken and only once
in the written version. A similar comparison
can be made for the use of the word he. In
other words, the first NNS describes the
process of going from the specifics of the
movie to the general message, the second NNS
does not. This may account for the fact that
the distinction between specific and generic,
reflected in a grammatical distinction, assumes
major importance in the text of the first NNS.

PROBLEM 5.3

Given the data in this problem, one can
define repetition as those instances in which
a lexical item or phrase is used at least
twice within X words. The decision of how
to analyze data of this sort is, in a sense,
an arbitrary one. One could, of course,
assign a value of any number to X. To ade-
quately capture the nature of repetition in
these data one might want to include semantic

repetitions rather than just exact word
repetition. For example, "the man works at
the tribal office; that's where he works."
The underlined portion clearly refers to the
preceding utterance. It also appears to have
an emphatic effect. It is not dissimilar to
the effect in the next sentence "and my wife,
and my 'wife" or "... my wife is no good. and
my wife is no good" in which there are examples
of exact repetition.

The quantification of the data in Part II
depends on the definition which is established
in Part I. What is necessary, however, is for
students, in as principled a way as possible,
to determine the domain in which repetition
occurs (25 words, 50 words, the whole composition, etc.) and whether or not an exact
repetition must occur. If not, how much
semantic and/or syntactic similarity must
there be?

There are examples of repetition in these
data (again, how this is quantified will
depend on the a priori decisions which the
students make) which seem unlike what happens
in written English compositions. For example,
the phrase she will be in great need of some-
one who loves her is repeated, as is she will
be left alone (she will be alone). In comparing the IL data with NL data there are two
caveats: first, the comparison is between a
spoken and a written text and, second, one
would have to gather similar data from
a) other learners of English, and b) NS's of
English before one can conclude that rhetorical
transfer has taken place. That is, one would
want to make sure that it is not a learner
phenomenon, generalizable to all learners,
whatever the NL, and that it is not a fact

of English writing that promotes the kind of
repetition seen in Part II.

In Part III, transfer of different kinds of
lexical items are treated differentially.
Given Navajo society, we can assume that the
words in 1 are important in their culture and
are thus emphasized more by means of repetition
both in Navajo and in their L2 English. Thus,
transfer of the rhetorical strategy of
repetition does not appear to be a monolithic
phenomenon. Rather, Bartelt claims that it
is dependent on the meaning and the emotional
value of topics.

PROBLEM 5.4

While the first composition is for the most
part grammatically correct, there is a lack of
specificity in terms of anaphora. This con-
tributes to the infelicitous style relating to
clarity of reference. Consider the two sentences below:

a)   His mouth is upturned with thick
     lips and (*his mouth/he) has
     white clean teeth. (The words
     in parentheses would have had
     to be included to make clear
     the referent.)

b)   His body build is of normal shape
     *with (and he has) broad shoulders.

In the third sentence, the pupil has used the
instead of his:

c)   He is light in complexion and *the
     (his) whole body is covered with fur.

While the sentence is understandable, he
has failed to make the reference clear. This
is not necessarily a matter of knowing how to
express meaning or how to be precise. Rather,
this student has not learned English conven-
tions for anaphora, here relating to body
parts. The main problem in the second composition is again unclear reference, caused by
ambiguity of the reference of they to both
men and women (cf. particularly the second
paragraph). The only other error (vis à vis
the TL) appears in the first sentence of the
fifth paragraph.

The second composition differs from the
first in that the type of error has changed
from omission of reference items in the
first, to ambiguous reference in the second.

In the first composition of Part II, the
pupil has used the conjunction and frequently,
and the conjunctions as, because, and when only
once each. By contrast, in the second composition, and, but, because, than, as well all
appear in the first sentence alone. Thus,
simply in terms of quantity, there are far more
conjunctions used in the second composition
than in the first. One could argue that
this is because the second composition is
longer. However, this is not the case.
The number of conjunctions per sentence has
increased, too. Also, the second composition
contains a much greater variety of conjunctions than the first. As a result of
attempting to use many more different conjunctions, the possibility for error has
increased in the second composition. In
the first composition, there are no
mistakes in the conjunctions used, while
in the second, some conjunctions are used

inappropriately. For example, therefore in line 7 does not clearly establish a cause-effect relationship between that sentence and the preceding one.

PROBLEM 5.5

The data presented in this problem were also presented and analyzed in part in an earlier work (Chimombo 1979). We refer the reader to that article because it provides background information on the data presented here.

If code-switching is defined as a change from one language to another at sentence boundaries within one speaker's conversational turn, or when speakers change, the child switches a total of six times in Transcript 1.

1. oh, dolly's soap (p. 95)
2. I want a towel for dolly .... (p. 96)
3. daddy, go away .... (p. 96)
4. yeah it's OK .... (p. 96)
5. oh no, I don't .... (p. 97)
6. no/no (screaming) (p. 97)

Each time she responds to or comments on in Chichewa a prior English utterance by one of her parents. The parents attempt six times to bring the conversation back to Chichewa.

If code-switching includes the use of loan blends and phonetically unaltered loan words within one sentence, then we can also count the sentences including a) the word dolly (phonetically unaltered loan word; loan blend = chidole); b) the word sopo

(loan blend for soap); c) the word pinafore
(phonetically unaltered loan word, British
English for jumper).

There are three instances of dolly want —
rather than dolly wants, which could be either
developmental or NL-based. Chichewa makes no
suffixed distinction between first, second,
and third persons. There are a number of
indications that the "error" may be developmental. First, the child is young. Second,
there is a similarity to the other errors of
omission of tense markers, e.g., spill —
instead of spilled; I — stop you instead of
I'll stop you. These errors are similar to
those made by NL learners of English. One
could have argued that these were instances
of transfer from Chichewa if the child had
included the future marked will but not the
other tense markers, since in English the
future is one tense in which the marker
precedes the base form of the verb. It
seems that many of the errors of usage
may be due to the fact that they are absent
from Chichewa, thus being NL-based errors.
However, some could also be developmental.
Particularly likely to be NL-based are the
two instances where the child prefixes an
adjective (on its own) with an article,
possibly copying the Chichewa system of
concord between noun and adjective — interestingly, the two examples, "dolly is a all
dry" and "no, you're a naughty," both refer
to animate or pseudo-animate nouns, in
which case the English article is almost
homophonous with the marker for Chichewa
noun concord: "Dolly akulira?" and
"Akusamba, sakulira."

There is evidence that the child is losing
her first language in that she utters only
three complete sentences in Chichewa throughout
the conversation, and each of these sentences
uses the same verb, in the same form, waipitsa
which was first imitated from her mother
"Waipitsa ndani?" Only three different
Chichewa verbs are used, kumina, kugona, and
ipitsa, each present in her mother's prior
utterances. She also introduces English words
into Chichewa phrases, such as pa knee and pa
book. Her mother spends a lot of time and
effort unsuccessfully correcting errors of
concord between the noun and the possessive
marker, such as "zala ya" instead of "zala za"
and "mikono wa" instead of "mikono ya."
Finally, there is no real exchange of information in Chichewa; in other words, it is not a
conversation, whereas in English there is some
information exchange.

The child has great difficulty remembering
particular vocabulary items, e.g., a) knee
book; b) pronunciation of some words, e.g.,
mawondo; and c) noun concords for singular
and plural forms, e.g., zala izi, zala za,
mikono ya.

In the second transcript, the child utters
only three complete sentences in Chichewa, as
compared with nine in the first one, even
though both transcripts are approximately the
same length. Furthermore, the nine Chichewa
sentences in the first transcript are more
varied in both meaning and structure than the
three in the second: in the first transcript,
seven different verbs are used (ziziritsa,
sambitsa, funa, samba, lira, thira, bvula), as
compared with only three in the second (mina,
gona, ipitsa); these verbs appear in a greater

variety of forms (imperative, present continu-
ous, present simple, negative, infinitive, as
compared with infinitive and present perfect
in Transcript 2). Further, in the first
transcript they are not all immediate imitations of a prior utterance by the parents.
In the second they are immediate imitations.
In the first transcript there is no correction
of the child's utterances (in fact, there are
few errors, all of which are self-
corrected in a later utterance or which
appeared correctly earlier), while a large
part of the second transcript is taken up
by correction. Finally, there is a large
difference in the amount of information
exchanged. The first transcript is a real
conversation while the second turns into a
Chichewa grammar lesson — it is only when the
child switches to English that the communica-
tive function of language is restored.

PROBLEM 5.6

The TL descriptions for both of the
children are quite sparse, consisting primarily
of factual information. That is, the children
describe only what is in the picture. On the
other hand, the kind of information provided
by the NL descriptions is quite different.
The children include not only descriptive
information, but evaluative information as
well. For example, Child 1 begins with
The long awaited spring; Child 2 with It was a
beautiful spring day. There is more background
information (setting the scene) in the NL
pictures (the shining sun, the warm days, the
clouds in the sky, etc.). Another difference
can be seen in the amount of implicit and

explicit information between the two picture
descriptions. In Child 1's description there
is explicit mention in the TL description of
the picture of the existence of the garden:
there is a large garden. In the NL description, the garden is inferred by the fact that
the children are planting tomatoes, cucumbers,
onions, etc. While the difference is not as
striking for Child 2, that child also begins
with an explicit statement of the existence
of the garden, whereas in the NL description
the existence is assumed: The children have
come into their garden. A final difference
between the versions is that both children
use names for the children in the NL
descriptions (Azat, Rustam), but do not in
the TL versions.

Two caveats about these data are:
1) since the way the task was set up was not
available, one does not know how much of the
description was task-dependent. This,
however, is always a consideration in L2
acquisition research; 2) students should
be cautioned about using translations of
original data. In this case, given that the
question one was asking concerns content,
the use of translation does not seem un-
warranted. Thus, the appropriateness of
the data base (as in all L2 acquisition research) depends on the questions which are
asked.

PROBLEM 5.7

The data in this problem come from Harley
(1982). An important aspect of this work is
that it studies Toronto French-immersion
learners about ten years after the beginning

of the Immersion Program. It thus complements
the data presented in Problems 1.8, 2.2, 2.4,
and 2.5. An updated report on data from this
situation, including the all-important question of positive evidence for fossilization is
presented in Harley and Swain (1984). In
Harley (1982), she discusses modality and
polite requests in terms of both the French
verb system and the learner's task
(pp. 108 - 109), as well as the findings in
the context where students in each of the
five groups were specifically asked to make
a polite request (pp. 170 - 173), the topic
of this problem.

    The heart of the problem involves two
factors: a) the ability to express politeness
via the marked verb conditional form, and
b) the sociolinguistic error of addressing a
stranger with the highly familiar singular
form of the verb (the tu form). Concerning
factor (a), it appears that age is more
important than NL. This of course can only
be known when a comparison with NL baseline
data is made (cf. discussion in Problem 4.9
re Andersen 1983). Harley points out that
the ability to appropriately use this form
is not fully developed even by NS's at age
six and seven. Concerning factor (b), not
once in the data do the NS's make this
error, whereas the immersion students,
particularly the early ones, frequently do.
Harley attributes this to language transfer
effects, where the immersion students
addressing a stranger with the tu form, are
presumably influenced by the invariant you
form of English. Thus, we can see NNS
behavior as different from NS behavior.

    Comparing the younger and older native-
speaking children, both use second person

plural forms to express politeness (i.e., vous
not tu), but they differ in that the older
children regularly (8 out of 12) use the
conditional, e.g., Pardon, Monsieur, est-ce
que vous auriez l'heure, par hasard?;
... Est-ce que je pourais savoir l'heure ...;
or ... Est-ce que je pourais avoir l'heure ...,
etc.; whereas the younger children rarely do
(2 out of 12). The conclusion, if held up by
further study, that age and not NL is the
determining factor here is bolstered by the
fact, reported by Harley (p. 172), that there
is much less use of the conditional by younger
children in other contexts. Class discussion
could revolve around the factual status of
these claims, noting that the conditional for
politeness is used by none of the NNS's. All
the groups seem to use monsieur more or less
equally. In terms of the polite vous form,
none of the early immersion grade 1 students
(Group A) use it; it is hardly used at all by
the early partial immersion older children
(Group C); while the older late immersion
children (Group B) use it fairly frequently.
Comparing the groups more precisely would have
to take account of the number of times the
polite vous form is used related to the number
of times a second person context is provided by
the students in responding to the role-playing
question. Since role playing is widely used
in SLA research, class discussion could also
relate to the reasonableness of extracting
from this task to what one might do in naturally occurring discourse.

PROBLEM 5.8

In general, native English speakers tend to
offer apologies more than the other groups
(exceptions are the three situations with the

elderly lady). With one exception they also
offer an explanation more than the other
two groups. Each group accepts responsibility
to a greater extent than the others for
some situations, but not for others. Repair
is offered most frequently by native
English speakers. A promise of forebearance
is offered most frequently by native
Russian speakers. In comparing percentages
of NS's and learners, there is some indication of NL patterns being followed. For
example, in situation 1, native English
speakers had a pattern 92 - 42 - 100
(apology, explanation, and responsibility,
respectively) and IL patterns follow the
same relative order (69 - 23 - 92). While
the direction is the same, the precise
percentages are not. On the other hand,
in situation 4 the direction of the
results is not the same for either the
native English or native Russian groups
when comparing NL and IL responses. One
reason for the discrepancy in results may
have to do with the small number of subjects. In other words, the responses may
represent individual differences in
responses (e.g., based on personality
differences) as opposed to representing
real group trends. Another possible
reason for the lack of trend is that the
differences in apology types may be too
slight to be able to detect differences.

Because the differences are not easily
seen, it may be helpful to investigate the
average frequency across all situations.
The results (Olshtain 1983:245-247) are
as follows:

Average Frequency of Semantic Formulas
in Native Speech

	Eng.	Russ.	Heb.	Eng. in Heb.	Russ. in Heb.
Apology	80	70	56	72	71
Explana-tion	63	27	43	47	46
Responsi-bility	52	45	31	50	46
Repair	46	19	36	22	31
Forbear-ance	10	13	5	6	42
$\overline{X}$ =	50.2	34.8	34.2	39.4	47.2

In general, the English speakers decrease in
all five categories in the IL, whereas Russians
show an increase in all five categories.
Despite the decrease in the IL, in all cases
but one (repair), the English speakers still
apologize in Hebrew more than native Hebrew
speakers. Similarly, the Russian speakers in
all cases but one (repair) apologize to a
greater extent in their IL than native Hebrew
speakers. It may be that the native English
speakers infer a lesser amount of apology in
Hebrew. In the case of "repair," they "over-
shot" the TL norm and offered repair less in
their IL than either native English or native
Hebrew. Russian speakers, on the other hand,
may not have perceived such a difference (in
fact, overall there was very little difference,
34.8 vs. 34.2). A suggestion offered by
Olshtain is that the difference in the amount
of apology of the two groups is due to the

difference in social prestige of the two groups in the context of the study. English speakers may be trying to maintain a sense of cultural superiority, hence apologizing less, whereas Russians, in their effort to be accepted and liked, feel a greater need to apologize.

PROBLEM 6.1

The native speakers emphasize a particular lexical item (possibly with louder speech) (#1); they repeat a question with fronting to emphasize the important element (#2); they offer a possible answer in #3; they break the question into parts (#4 and #5); they offer a choice and accept an inappropriate response in #6; they repeat the question asking for slightly different information in #7.

All of these are examples in which the native speaker appears to assist the nonnative speaker in understanding a question so as to allow the conversation to proceed smoothly, even though at times inappropriately or unexpected TL norms are used.

PROBLEM 6.2

In #1 the response is a repetition with rising intonation; in #2 there is repetition with falling intonation; in #3 the NS finishes the question which the NNS had begun. In #4 there is a direct response to a question. In the responses to NNS's there seems to be a need to verify that the information has been correctly understood. There is also a delay

before responding. Perhaps this is a way
of gathering one's thoughts before entering
into what is likely to be a more difficult
exchange than usual. With the exception
of category 1, the responses to the more
advanced NNS's show a tendency to be
more similar to the NS's in that there
is less of a need to verify the correctness
of the interpretation. There is an
increase in direct responses and in repetition with falling intonation. Tradi-
tionally, FT is associated with notions of
loudness, shorter phrases, and simpler
phrases (cf. Hatch 1983:183 - 184 for an
excellent list of FT features). These
responses suggest that FT may best be considered within a broader framework, that is,
as any difference in the way NS's address
NNS's in comparison with the ways they
address other NS's. This expanded definition fits in with Long's (1980) distinction
between modified input and modified interaction.

PROBLEM 6.3

NS's appear to hedge; there are more
qualifiers and softeners such as kind of,
that's close, somewhat, I could go along,
basically, and so forth. On the other hand,
NNS's are more direct: I am agree; I changed
my mind; we are agree. As with the expression of agreement, NS's offer more hedges
and softeners such as I wouldn't necessarily
agree with that; kind of; I was very
arbitrary; whereas NNS's are direct in their
expression of disagreement: I no agree;
I disagree; is wrong.

PROBLEM 6.4

In #1 content is corrected; in #2 a lexical item is corrected; in #3 a grammatical form (<u>angles</u>) is corrected; and in #4 a grammatical form is corrected (<u>when he finishes</u>). In #1 the correction is made in a direct manner, whereas in #2, #3, and #4 the correction is made indirectly by merely stating the correct form. A possible explanation is that the NS is direct in making a correction of content because that is a mistake that anyone (NS or NNS) could make. On the other hand, the correction is indirect, and hence more gentle in situations where it is due to a language deficiency on the part of the NNS since this type of error is due to a knowledge deficit and not an error that can be made by anyone. The issue of corrections "working" is a difficult one to deal with. For example, in #2 and #3 the NNS repeats the correct form, yet how does one know whether the information was assimilated and whether the forms will be used correctly at a later time. It may be that repetition of this sort only represents an ability to repeat from short-term memory and does not represent incorporation into the IL system.

PROBLEM 6.5

In #1 there seems to be little connection in the discourse. There are abrupt topic shifts. In #2 the topics are connected with information flowing naturally from one to another. The conversation in #3 is similar in some respects to #1 and in other respects to

#2. The beginning of the conversation is
similar to the conversation in #1 in that the
participants are searching for common ground.
As the conversation progresses the participants
have established a common subject area and the
conversation flows freely.

<u>PROBLEM 6.6</u>

The NNS's indicate non-understanding by
direct means (1,3,6), by indirect means
(2,4,5,6,8), by silence (7), and by summarizing (9). There are two ways of accounting
for the indications of non-understandings in
Part II. One could claim that there are more
instances of non-understandings in NNS/NNS
conversations and that is why there are more
overt indications of such. On the other hand,
one could argue that NNS's feel more comfor-
table in conversations with other NNS's and
feel less "embarrassed" to ask for clarifica-
tion. In other words, it is not that there <u>is</u>
less understanding, but that the participants
are more willing to let their interlocutor
know that they have not understood. One could
argue that there is a mutually recognized
"incompetence" in the domain of English which
provides an unembarrassing forum in which to
express one's "ignorance," something learners
cannot easily do in conversations with NS's
in which they are not on equal footing.

Of the four groups there seems to be a
progression from <u>least</u> negotiation of meaning
(and hence presumably greatest understanding)
for those groups where there is the greatest
amount of shared background (language and
proficiency level) and the <u>most</u> negotiation

of meaning where there is the least shared
background (no shared language and no shared
proficiency level).

The sentences read by an individual subject
consist of an ungrammatical and a grammatical
version of the same sentence. In general, the
grammatical version of a sentence is judged as
having better pronunciation than the ungrammatical version (cf. for example subject 1 — the
grammatical version [#20] had 26 "good"
responses and one "bad" response, whereas the
ungrammatical version [#1] had eight "good"
and 19 "bad" responses). Thus, one's pronunciation is in part determined by the grammaticality of an utterance. In general, one can
hypothesize that this is related to the
general notion of comprehensibility. Pronunciation and grammaticality are counterbalancing
factors in the total picture of comprehensibility of NNS speech.

In Part II one can determine the sentences
which are easiest to understand by means of a
ratio of (number of words correct)/(total
number of words). [A syllable count would
also be an appropriate means for determining
ease of understanding.] One can infer from
Part I that some speakers (e.g., #10 and #3)
had poor pronunciation which may have inter-
fered significantly with understanding since,
regardless of the grammaticality of the sentence, the responses were predominantly "bad."
The NS had difficulty understanding these
speakers, as can be seen by her response to
those sentences in comparison with others.

The kindergarten teacher in question appears to address the children differently depending on their English language proficiency. For example, the teacher addresses the children in #1 and the child in #2 (NS's) with complete sentences. In #1 there is an example of an embedded sentence and a conjoined sentence. In #2 there is an example of adjective stacking. In #3, in which a NNS is addressed, the teacher breaks the adjectives into two sentences, most likely separated by a pause (cf. <u>a great big pointed hat</u> vs. <u>hat is big. Pointed.</u>). In #4 a NNS of even lower proficiency is addressed with simpler lexical items (<u>big and tall</u> vs. <u>pointed</u>) and in #5, speaking to the lowest proficiency child, the teacher repeats only one adjective (<u>big</u>).

The data in A confirm the conclusions of Part I. The teacher speaks differently to different children, and a progression can be seen based on the proficiency levels of the children. She speaks with greater frequency to the low-level child and the least to the low-medium-level child than to the medium-level child. On the other hand, the mean length of utterance (MLU) is in the reverse order (lowest MLU to least proficient and highest MLU to most proficient). The NS does not fit the progression in the percentage of teacher utterances. However, one can imagine that the language needs of the children in some way interact with the instructional needs.

In B we see that the type/token ratio is low for the low-level student. Hence, the lexical items addressed to that student did not vary much. The ratio suggests that there

is an increase in the variety of words used as
a function of the NNS's increased proficiency.

In general, one can claim that the teacher
skillfully adjusted her speech as a function
of a given child's language abilities. This
was presumably done in an effort to aid the
child in understanding, for the purpose of
both language acquisition and content learning.

PROBLEM 7.1

If repetition (cf. also Problem 5.3) were
to mean repeating exact words, then there
clearly are examples in the text: e.g.,
acceleration, schedule, faster, and show to
the owner. The more interesting type of
repetition in this excerpt, however, involves
paraphrase. For example, in his first turn,
L talks about "accelerate the project" as
"use ... overtime ... instead of work eight
hours a day you can work ... ten hours or
twelve hours ...". In his sixth turn, he
mentions "make the project move faster as you
have to pay ... more labor more materials"
(see also turn 8). Note that the idea of
acceleration meaning "makes the project go
faster" is provided to the informant (turn 2)
by the cooperative interviewer in a summary
statement. Note also that one has to show to
the owner (turn 6) "why is more expensive"
and "why you espent more money ...".

The exact numbers L uses for an example
(i.e., as specific details for his generalization) are worth contemplating. First (turn 1),
"instead of work eight hours a day you can
work ten hours or twelve hours" compared with

(turn 8), "instead of use for example ten
laborers you have to use fifteen or twenty."
Though the numbers are higher, there appears
to be no new information provided rhetorically.
There are other possibilities for repetition.

Concerning exactly throughout these tapes,
L, after saying this word, often pauses and
then disagrees with the informant. Here (turns
2 and 3) L disagrees directly: "I think it's
no acceleration in this case." Note, inciden-
tally, that at times L uses you to specifically
refer to the contractor (or subcontractor),
but at other times it appears to be the normal
TL paraphrase for one.

To answer the final question in the problem, one must distinguish rhetorical strategies that appear in many types of texts (in
this case, general vs. specific information,
repetition, disagreement strategies and, in
the next two problems, such things as definition, mitigation, and word search) from
information structure (in this case, the
meaning of acceleration and what is involved in
the construction process).

PROBLEM 7.2

In the engineering episode, the interviewer
S uses the wrong technical term from the point
of view of L, the informant, the "knower" of
the technical information in spite of being
the NNS. The interviewer, in an effort to
help move the conversation along, had suggested
as an exemplary construction model a structure
where columns had to be built before the floor
could be put in. At first, L tries to use his

coparticipant's model in his explanation:
"goes goes in this way ...". But he soon
realizes that not only was the order of the
activities wrong, one cannot put in the
columns first ..., but also the terminology
itself needs correction: "but when you're
doing this you can make you put the the the
floor already on the foundations." He then
makes the correction without mitigation:
"let's say that this is foundations ...",
i.e., without giving the interviewer a face-
saving way out. Note that, when asked (see
quote in question 3) in the playback session
why he had corrected the interviewer at this
point, he confirms his technical stance "but
I didn't explaim him." Note that this second-
ary data from the playback session is valuable
because it provides information about the
coparticipants' structuring of the event.

In the matching nontechnical episode, L is
talking with a different interviewer, P, an old
friend, about much more casual matters, the
preparation of food. He is describing a
northern Mexican dish and the particular
preparation of the meat that goes into it.
Here, in a parallel rhetorical mode, we see
the interviewer making a technical error, in
this case confusing tacos with burritos, but
this time L uses a politeness strategy in his
correction: "you mean like burritos?"
However, this mitigation causes even more
confusion and the interviewer suggests that,
where the meat is used in tacos in some parts
of the country, in Sonora it is used in
burritos. At this point, L becomes more
direct and explains that tacos are tacos in
his part of Mexico. "No, it's tacos," but
that in the dish in question, burritos are
used: "with that kind of meat you you you do

burritos." It might be suggested that, while
L was sure of his engineering domain and in
control of it, here he is less sure of the
nature of the domain, and may in fact be
attempting to negotiate the boundaries and
structure of it with his coparticipant.

PROBLEM 7.3

This pair of episodes illustrates the
informant's (1) abilities to deal with missing
vocabulary in the two domains discussed in
Problem 7.2: the technical (cost or control
engineering) and the nontechnical (preparation
of food). In the first episode (the domain
of engineering talk) the interviewer, S, had
asked L about reasons for construction equipment breaking down. Here L, the "expert/
knower" in spite of being the NNS in an NS/NNS
interaction situation, is able to carry on in
spite of the missing word. His strategy is to
describe the process involved in moving equipment from one part of the country to another
and the consequent effect on the performance
of the equipment. This episode shows how he
gets along, in a communication strategy sense,
in the face of a forgotten term: he continues
talking until he is able to access a synonym,
height, which allows his coparticipant to
suggest the correct English term. And then
they are both able to cooperate in summarizing
L's main point.

In the matching (nontechnical) episode, L
is again talking with the same interviewer, P,
as in Problem 7.2. Again, as in the technical
episode, L forgets a word. Although L appears
to be able to carry on in spite of the missing

item, there is much more of a breaking down,
where he produces the phrase forget it. This
contrasts with his performance in the technical
episode, where no such breakdowns occur. Note
that after the breakdown he attempts the same
communication strategy as in the technical
domain, using the rhetorical strategy of
describing a process leading up to a synonym
escramble for the missing term, then accepting
the term from the coparticipant, but it does
not succeed. In this episode, L struggles to
remember the word, even mentioning that he
learned it at the supermarket, "Farmer Jack,"
and attempts to break off the episode: forget
it. Only when his coparticipant suggests a
wrong word does he begin to employ the communication strategy and describe the process of
drying the meat and hitting it with a stone,
waiting for the coparticipant to offer another
correct term. The interviewer finally does
suggest mash, which L accepts as the correct
term. Selinker and Douglas (to appear) suggest
that the strategy failed in the end to achieve
the communication goal — exactly the correct
word from the coparticipant. They conclude:

> It is our belief that mash is not
> in fact the correct technical term L
> wanted to convey the meaning he
> sought — an action of crushing,
> grinding, and separating the dried
> meat, which is the process of making
> machaca. Probably no such word exists
> in English.

Here exactly as opposed to its use in
Problem 7.1 appears more TL-like, that is,
signifying agreement. L follows it up by continuing to discuss the process of making
machaca.

The sexist issue implied in question 5 is a difficult one to deal with. Selinker and Douglas state:

> We have been chided by some colleagues for creating a sexist issue here by having L talk technically to a male and about cooking to a female. On the one hand, it is hard for two male researchers to mount a defense on this issue and, eventually, we should, we suppose, try to "tease apart" sex variables from discourse domain variables. However, in this case we feel that part of the definition of discourse domains has to do with the particular audience involved. Evidence that this in fact is the case arises from the fact that we did not instruct the second interviewer to talk about food, but that the topic came up "naturally" in the interaction of the male/female coparticipants.

It is interesting that in the format of engineering talk L relies exclusively on verbal strategies to get his meaning across. Throughout the engineering talk in these interviews, L maintains a highly passive, emotionless posture while talking about his subject matter, where he is the expert/knower. This is in sharp contrast with the other domain, where his performance is full of expression, gesture, and movement. There thus appears to be a correlation between gesture and the various strategies discussed for Problems 7.1 through 7.3 An interesting class discussion could ensue here and teachers may wish to obtain the composite videotape underlying these transcripts.

PROBLEM 7.4

The concept of rhetorical "safe rules" is introduced, defined, and examples are given. These are "teaching data." "Learning data," in this case IL data, were gathered from compositions written in a pre-English for Academic Purposes (EAP) course in an ESL intensive program. All compositions (including first draft, second draft and, in some cases, third drafts) written in this eight-week course are included in the data set. Details about the learning and teaching data are given in Selinker (forthcoming).

The heart of this problem involves the bringing together of learning/teaching data and the argumentation needed to attribute changes in learning data due to a teaching experience. Such argumentation needs to be as precise as possible, since it is probably impossible to show incorporation of new learning into an IL system, since clearly it is a long-term affair. In the short term of most teaching experiences, what one can show are changes in learner behavior (learning data) which correspond to predictions generated by analyzing teaching data.

In this case two safe rules are concerned: topic statement of a paragraph, and comparison and contrast development of that topic statement. In the composition course involved, these rules are explicitly taught and students

are then asked to write a composition. In
terms of the original composition in Part I,
no topic statement is provided by the learner;
it is implicit. A conference is held with the
student, the safe rule is reviewed, and the
student's main point is brought out orally.
In the rewrite the student provides his core
idea not in terms of a topic statement but
as a summary. This is discouraged as being
"unsafe," however, since the reader has to
wait for the end of the paragraph to get the
main idea and may be led astray. Additionally, no hint of rhetorical development of
the paragraph can be provided after this
rhetorical choice. In terms of safe rule 2
in the original to Part I, method (a) is
chosen of comparing point by point in pairs,
and it seems quite successful in that the
intended comparisons and contrasts are understood as such. Little rewriting is needed
here with the explicit connective word
instead appearing in rewrite 1.

The original composition in Part II shows
change (acquisition?) in terms of safe rule 1,
in that a clear topic statement is provided
with a hint of developments, i.e., we will
discuss "positive ways" (X) first and "negative
ways" (Y) second. The rewrite shows that this
rhetorical choice of classification is made
even more explicit. Safe rule 2 is followed
in that choice (b) occurs, i.e., X and Y are
discussed in blocks, with all of the comparative details written for X first and then for
Y. In terms of explicit connectives, the
original in Part II shows no contrastive connective dividing discussion of X from
discussion of Y. This is remedied in rewrite
1 by the insertion of however in the proper
place. Also, the paragraph break is helpful

here should the writer wish to provide more
"negative aspects." Note the useful addition
of <u>moreover</u> in the development of Y, explicitly
showing the addition of another negative point.
Presumably rewrite 2, if needed, could have
aimed for the grammatical goal of only complete
sentences, but the student's rhetorical
choices were successful here.

In the composition in Part III, the last
one this computer engineering student wrote for
the course, the student tries to explain two
complicated but basic concepts in his field
through a comparison and contrast structure.
In terms of safe rule 1, he does not provide
an explicit topic statement. Instead, he immediately describes the concept, <u>bit</u>. In
terms of safe rule 2, he explicitly shows,
through the use of <u>however</u>, that he is con-
trasting <u>address</u> with <u>bit</u>. Note the complica-
tion for safe writing here in that "address"
in the student's conception of things is
specified by <u>characters</u> which are then related
to <u>bits</u>. Note the explicit contrastive connective word <u>yet</u>. Class discussion could
concentrate on this widely used connective and
how to explain its use, for it is one of the
hardest words to teach if the learning of it
implies knowing how to use it appropriately.
Finally, it appears clear that, at times,
teaching data as input made a difference in
this learner's writing.

PROBLEM 7.5

These original data by Rounds show the
interrelatedness of IL use and subject matter
concerns. Part I: in TA 1's class, a student

asks the TA to explain a problem. The TA
reads it and opens with a number of questions
aimed at getting the students to think; for
example, "What's the variable we can change?"
TA 2, on the other hand, approaches the task
as something he has to do, rather than something the group has to understand; for
example, "I want to finish Section 4.4."
Note that TA 2 asks no questions before getting
into the problem. Unlike TA 1, he does not
even ask if there are any questions about the
problem or even about the solution.

Concerning the data in Part II, the number
of turn changes is striking: for TA 1 there
are 23 turns, whereas for TA 2 there are only
three. After noting that the answer arrived
at (Part II) was a minimum, TA 1 sums up in
Part III with a discussion of which of two
ways one can determine if some point is a
maximum or if a minimum is preferable. TA 2,
on the other hand, ends the solution of the
last part of his problem (Part III) with "so
that's that problem ..." and does not try to
summarize. Instead he immediately moves to
another problem which again he introduces:
"This section is ... in 27 you have eh you
have ...". Note that TA 2 seems to have lots
more incomplete sentences which result in a
loss of information, e.g., "and eh that's
called ...".

In general, TA 1 depends more on his students to raise questions and allows for negotiation of explanation through a lot of turn
taking. TA 2, on the other hand, produces more
of a monologue and appears to take all the responsibility for introducing the material and
getting to the solution, i.e., he allows for
little student involvement in the task at hand.

PROBLEM 7.6

This problem comes from a trial where the
Filipino nurses were at first convicted.
Naylor believes that the conviction was directly attributable to crosslinguistic misunderstanding and especially to the transference of
the NL tense/aspect system to the IL. In Part
I we have the issue of possible perjury since
we have an apparent contradiction: "I would
say we are good friends" vs. "I don't know her
and we don't know each other that much." The
point here for Naylor is that

> this answer might have been true
> in the past ... therefore phrased in
> the present tense, the statement was
> false, and apparently a contradiction
> of the earlier testimony.

Naylor calls this

> aspect-related interference
> which may account for the apparent
> intent of the defendants to actually
> mislead the jury about what happened
> at the time of her alleged poisonings.

All this appears to come about because
of the wrong choice of the tense form of the
English verb, i.e., the nurses were constantly
using present tense forms for an intended
past tense meaning. There is clear evidence
for this in Part II "... What I know about
Pavulon in the summer of '75 ..." The
next exchanges are particularly revealing:

> what I <u>know</u> about Pavulon at the
> present time;

what you <u>knew</u> about Pavulon at that
    time;

I <u>know</u> a little about Pavulon

In the context, the last remark is clearly
ambiguous from a TL perspective. Note how the
prosecutor interprets it.

The examples in Part III illustrate the
difference between the nurse as defendant
being questioned and the prosecutor in terms
of the aspectual meaning carried by the English
verb forms <u>arrived</u>, <u>came</u>, <u>looked</u>, and
<u>discontinued</u>. Naylor attributes this to
language transfer, phrased in contrastive
analysis terms:

> The Tagalog equivalents of these
> verbs are punctual in aspectual mean-
> ing ... In English, on the other
> hand, these verbs may be durative —
> the act extending to the state.

This in turn may have had very important real-
life consequences in the murder trial:

> This mismatch of the aspectual
> range of verbs of this type in
> English and in Tagalog may underlie
> the failure of the defendants to
> establish clearly what their move-
> ments were during the emergencies
> they were alleged to have created.

The example of the extensive use of <u>I be-</u>
<u>lieve</u> is interesting since at times its use is
clearly inappropriate in a TL sense and its
overuse could easily leave negative impressions
on the all-important audience for this

testimony — the jury. Naylor finds no direct
contrastive analysis answer to this overuse
and raises two hypotheses: 1) the misuse of
the term in the sense of generalizing the meaning to include meanings of other words such as
I think, I guess, and even I conclude, and
2) a cultural hedge, i.e., "part of the norm
of indirectness that appears to characterize
interactions within Filipino culture." Though
why the particular form I believe is chosen is
not clear.

Questions 7 and 8 should lead to a class
discussion concerning the care which analysts
must take in interpreting the meaning of IL
utterances — see also Problem 4.2 (Corder
1981). The methodological problems of getting
at those meanings are far from resolved, but
playback techniques (cf. discussions to
Problems 7.1 through 7.3) have proven useful.

PROBLEM 8.1

The following are ways of categorizing the
sentences as containing restrictive (R) or
nonrestrictive (NR) relative clauses:

1.	NR	5.	NR	9.	NR
2.	R and NR	6.	NR	10.	NR
3.	R	7.	R	11.	R
4.	R	8.	R	12.	R

It is to be noted that these are only possible
categorizations. The major criterion used is
a semantic one: does the relative clause
restrict the domain of possible referents?
The semantic criterion is only one of the
criteria used in standard English for

determining relative clause types. Others are
orthography (nonrestrictive relative clauses
are separated from the main clause by commas),
the relative pronoun (that) cannot be used in
nonrestrictive relatives, restrictions on the
noun phrase being modified (proper names
cannot take restrictive relatives without
making them generic, as in "That's not the
Sally Jones that I used to know"). This problem illustrates the general difficulty in
dealing with IL data when categories of TL (or
NL) are used by the analyst. The IL categories are not always the same as NL or TL
categories. The researcher is thus imposing
his/her system on the data, the result often
being that the real pattern of the data is
obscured (see also Problem 1.5). For example,
Kumpf (1984) found that tensing on verbs by a
Japanese learner of English was not used to
mark completed action, but rather is used for
stative verbs and noncompleted action. This
differs from both the NL and the TL systems.
An open question is whether there are categories in IL's which do not occur in other
(natural) languages.

Another methodological issue which this
problem raises is that of interpreting a
speaker's intent. Particularly in sentence
level analyses of this sort, it is difficult
to determine what the speaker intended to say.
This becomes even more problematic when a major
criterion for analysis is meaning.

PROBLEM 8.2

This experimental design is weak in a number
of respects. The researcher, henceforth (R),
did not control for the NL of the subjects.

Neither did the R control for the teacher's individual style of teaching. For example, the teachers may have used different ways of giving explanations. Some may have used more extensive drill than others. Also, the type of drill used was not specified and instructors may have spoken different dialects. Since each teacher scored his/her own students' tests, there was a built-in bias, since they may have become "used" to a particular pronunciation. Apparently no information was gathered about how much contact the students had outside of the classroom in the form of TL-speaking friends, T.V., movies, tutors, etc. There was no indication of age of the subjects and educational level. The test which originally placed students in one of three proficiency levels was not based on pronunciation. Yet, the design of the experiment is dependent on three different levels of pronunciation abilities. It is easy to imagine a grammatically proficient student whose pronunciation abilities are weak and vice versa. Collecting data at two points in time does not necessarily mean that the path followed in between was a direct line. Consider the three possibilities shown in the diagram on page 100. In (a) the lab group and the class group followed two different paths. Had the testing been done before the point of crossover, a different result would have obtained. One could make the same claim about the graph in (b). Only in (c) is there an implication of linearity. The results would have been the same wherever sampled. Only the magnitude of difference would differ (cf. Kellerman, 1985, for a discussion of U-shaped behavior in L2 acquisition).

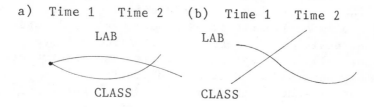

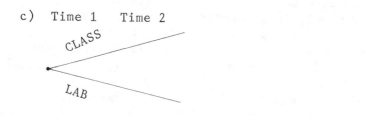

There are still other factors which
could have contributed to the differences
found. The amount of homework is not specified. How much correction was there in
class? Were the groups equally motivated?
How long had the subjects been in a TL com-
munity? Had some of them been in a TL-
speaking environment for some time, their
pronunciation may have fossilized, whereas
others may be at a point of new learning
(cf. Gass 1984 for a discussion of new
phonetic learning). How many times did the
teacher listen to the tape? The more s/he
listened to it, the better s/he may have been
at picking out errors. The analysis did not
consist of an analysis by level. There may
have been different results for different
levels. There are too many other factors which
could have contributed to the results to
warrant the conclusion which the R came to.

PROBLEM 8.3

From the utterances in Part I, one would assume that the learner is having difficulty with prepositions. However, in Part II we see that the student claims to have difficulty not with prepositions but with tense usage. This problem thus illustrates the inappropriateness of equating error and difficulty. Difficulty is a concept which implies some sort of struggle on the part of the learner in dealing with TL data. On the other hand, an error is an overt manifestation of a system which is not target-like. The error may or may not have resulted from "difficulty" or a "struggle" with the TL system. This clearly relates to the product (error)/process (difficulty) distinction made in L2 research.

PROBLEM 8.4

The rank order of errors for each grammatical category differs depending on task type. The translation task and picture description tasks are similar in that prepositions and pronouns are ranked 1 and 2, respectively, and determiners exhibit the lowest error percentage. However, the exact percentages differ. Errors in the free conversion task have relatively equal distribution among the five grammatical categories. In this task the learners are more able to "avoid" those areas which they know are problem areas for them and hence errors of particular types (e.g., prepositions) may be less likely to appear in the data. In the other tasks the language demands are controlled by the researcher and not by the learner. Furthermore, the learner is able to "monitor" his/her production to a greater or lesser extent on different tasks.

If results vary depending on task demands, then one is limited in the conclusions that can be drawn based on data from a single elicitation measure. Thus, the generalizability of such results is limited (cf. Tarone 1979 and 1982 for a fuller discussion of this issue).

PROBLEM 8.5

Subject 1's control of direct object (DO) pronouns appears TL-like. Subjects 2 and 3 appear not to control DO pronouns in TL fashion. They appear to have a rule which does not include anaphoric pronouns in the second clause of a sentence (there is one exception for each). Subject 4 has better control than subjects 2 and 3, although it is not TL-like. Subject 1 appears to be the most advanced since all forms are congruent with expected TL norms.

In the data presented in Part II, subject 1's usage is variable. It appears that an anaphoric pronoun is not used if it was used in the immediately preceding discourse. The other three subjects' usage of DO pronouns is TL-like in all cases (there is one agreement error for subject 3 in utterance 6).

In Part III all subjects exhibited correct usage of DO pronouns. The three elicitation procedures can be seen to represent a progression from one in which a great deal of attention was paid to speech (Part I) to a lesser amount of attention paid to speech (Part II), to the least amount in Part III. These differences contribute to the

differential results found in these data (cf.
Problem 3.4, in which there is the least
amount of accuracy in free conversation). As
in the preceding problem, one must be alert to
the fact that different results are obtained
based on the particular elicitation measure
used. In reporting and analyzing research
results, care must be taken to consider all
aspects of data collection, including the
conditions under which data were gathered and
the method used to gather them (cf. Tarone
1979).

PROBLEM 8.6

In #1 the NNS responds with an appropriate
answer (no ... no). In #2 there is a confirma-
tion check followed by an appropriate response
(sharp? no) and then an affirmative response
to the question Is it smooth?. In #3 the NNS
responds negatively and appropriately. In #4
the conversation proceeds smoothly, the only
"difficulty" stemming from the fact that the
NNS has forgotten the word knife. In #5,
after some prompting, the NNS asks the question,
as the NS wants. In #6 the NNS responds with
confidence that it is not to eat. In #7 there
has apparently been a misunderstanding surrounding the phrase one whole day. Yet, the
conversation proceeds with each person taking
an appropriate turn. It is because of the
appropriateness of the turns (most likely
without hesitation and with apparent confidence) that the misunderstanding goes unrecog-
nized.

It is clear from the retrospection data
that where there appeared to be understanding,

as suggested by the reasonableness and
appropriateness of the responses, there in
fact was not understanding. For example, in
#4 it seemed clear (to an analyst) from the
conversation that the NNS knew what the object
was, but lacked the word knife. Yet the
retrospection data clearly show that the NNS
did not have the object in mind, but did know
the word knife. The data in this problem
show that a) there can be discrepancies in
the way an analyst and a participant view a
conversation, and that b) conversations can
continue despite the fact that communication
in the sense of meaning exchange does not
take place (cf. Varonis and Gass, in press,
for an extended example).

PROBLEM 8.7

The Arabic, Farsi, and Chinese speakers use
pronominal copies (PC) in genitive and indirect
object position, but not in subject position
(cf. #2). Arabic and Farsi speakers use PC's
in DO position and Arabic speakers in object
of comparative position. These data suggest
that learners use IL pronominal copies in
just those places in which the NL has PC's.

The data in Part II show that speakers of
languages without PC's in relative clauses use
them in some relative clause positions (object
of comparative and genitive) but not in others
in their IL. If one considers both sets of
data, it is clear that an explanation of
transfer is appropriate in one set but not in
another. In fact, there are universal principles, based on hierarchical orderings of
relative clauses (see Keenan and Comrie 1977),

which would predict that languages of the world are more likely to have PC's in some positions (e.g., object of comparative) than others (e.g., subject). If there is some psychological reality to the hierarchy (cf. Keenan 1975) such that some positions are more "difficult" than others, then we would expect this to be reflected in IL's, as in fact is the case in Part II. Thus, in order to argue for transfer, one must have not only data which show influence of the NL in the IL, but also data from speakers of languages in which one can demonstrate a lack of NL influence in cases where the NL does not have the feature in question. Because a form from the NL appears in the IL does <u>not</u> necessarily mean that transfer has taken place. Other explanations are possible. In this regard one can also raise the issue of multiple causation in IL (cf. Zobl 1980).

PROBLEM 8.8

This problem is related to Problem 4.9 and the fuller data set in Appendix I. The important methodological point here is that the <u>unattested forms</u> in B of the data show that postverbal units of the type in A — Object, Time, Place, and Adverb strings — are not broken in IL data; thus, these are <u>the</u> units of IL word order in this case. The "non-breaking" of units in IL data is a result found elsewhere in the literature (cf., e.g., Ellis 1982). Clearly, this does not necessarily mean that in every case the units of NL or TL analysis equal those of IL analysis (see Problem 8.1 and Long and Sato 1984 for discussion).

The NL data in C directly parallel the IL
data with NL word order units being bounded
in the same way. This result adds evidence to
the reasonableness of the IL word order units
set up. Question 4 is quite interesting (the
factual observation comes from Helmut Zobl,
p.c.). If it is the case that the transfer of
Time-Place word order from the L1 is wide-
spread and persistent, then first of all this
argues even more strongly for the reality of
IL units of Time and Place; secondly, this
potential of IL learning should reinforce the
transfer claims made for the particular case
under study in Problem 4.9 and the related
data in Appendix I.

REFERENCES[1]

Adjemian, C. 1976. On the nature of interlanguage systems. Language Learning. 26.
297 - 320.
Bailey, N., C. Madden, and S. Krashen. 1974.
Is there a "natural sequence" in adult
second language learning? Language
Learning. 24. 235 - 243.
Beebe, L. In press. Input: Choosing the
right stuff. In S. Gass and C. Madden
(eds.) Input in Second Language Acquisi-
tion. Rowley, Mass.: Newbury House.
Chimombo, M. 1979. An analysis of the order
of acquisition of English grammatical
morphemes in a bilingual child. Working
Papers in Bilingualism. 18. 201 - 230.
Clements, G. and S. J. Keyser. 1983. CV
Phonology: a Generative Theory of the
Syllable. Cambridge: MIT Press.
Corder, S. P. 1973. Introducing Applied Lin-
guistics. Harmondsworth: Penguin.
Corder, S. P. 1981. Error Analysis and
Interlanguage. Oxford: Oxford University
Press.
Corder, S. P. 1983. A role for the mother
tongue. In S. Gass and L. Selinker (eds.),
Language Transfer in Language Learning.
Rowley, Mass.: Newbury House.
Dulay, H. and M. Burt. 1974. Natural sequen-
ces in child second language acquisition.
Language Learning. 24. 37 - 54.

[1]Full references are included only for references not cited in the Workbook.

Dvorak, T. 1983. Subject-object reversals in the use of gustar among New York Hispanics. In L. Elias-Olivares (ed.). Spanish in the U.S. Setting: Beyond the Southwest. Rosslyn, Virginia: NCBE.

Dvorak, T. and C. Kirshner. 1982. Mary like fishes: Reverse psychological phenomena in New York Puerto Rican Spanish. Bilingual Review. 9. 59 - 65.

Ellis, R. 1982. The origins of interlanguage. Applied Linguistics. 3. 207 - 223.

Gass, S. 1983. The development of L2 intuitions. TESOL Quarterly. 17. 273 - 291.

Gass, S. and L. Selinker. 1983. Language Transfer in Language Learning. Rowley, Mass.: Newbury House.

Hanania, E. and H. Gradman. 1977. Acquisition of English structures: A case study of an adult native speaker of Arabic in an English-speaking environment. Language Learning. 27. 75 - 92.

Harley, B. and M. Swain. 1984. The interlanguage of immersion students and its implication for second language teaching. In A. Davies and C. Criper (eds.). Interlanguage: Papers in Honour of S. Pit Corder. Edinburgh: University of Edinburgh Press.

Jain, M. 1969. Error analysis of an Indian English corpus. ms. University of Edinburgh.

Jain, M. 1974. Error analysis: source, cause and significance. In J. Richards (ed.). Error Analysis: Perspectives on Second Language Acquisition. London: Longman.

Keenan, E. 1975. Variation in universal grammar. In R. Fasold and R. Shuy (eds.). Analyzing Variation in Language. Washington, D.C.: Georgetown University Press.

Keenan, E. and B. Comrie. 1977. Noun phrase
    accessibility and universal grammar.
    Linguistic Inquiry. 8. 63 - 99.
Kellerman, E. 1985. If at first you do
    succeed .... In S. Gass and C. Madden
    (eds.), Input in Second Language Acquisi-
    tion. Rowley, Mass.: Newbury House.
Long, M. 1980. Input, Interaction and Second
    Language Acquisition. Ph.D. Dissertation.
    UCLA.
Long, M. and C. Sato. 1984. Methodological
    issues in interlanguage studies: an
    interactionist perspective. In A. Davies
    and C. Criper (eds.), Interlanguage:
    Papers in Honour of S. Pit Corder.
    Edinburgh: University of Edinburgh Press.
Rosansky, E. 1976. Methods and morphemes in
    second language acquisition research.
    Language Learning. 26. 409 - 426.
Selinker, L. 1972. Interlanguage. IRAL. 10.
    210 - 231.
Selinker, L. Forthcoming. Safe rules in
    ESL/EFL Theory and Interlanguage.
Selinker, L. 1984. Current issues in inter-
    language: An attempted critical summary.
    In A. Davies and C. Criper (eds.),
    Interlanguage: Papers in Honour of S. Pit
    Corder. Edinburgh: University of
    Edinburgh Press.
Selkirk, E. In press. Phonology and Syntax:
    The Relation between Sound and Structure.
    Cambridge, Mass.: MIT Press.
Tarone, E. 1974. A discussion of the "Dulay
    and Burt" studies. Working Papers in
    Bilingualism. 4. 16 - 27.
Tarone, E. 1979. Interlanguage as chameleon.
    Language Learning. 29. 181 - 191.
Tarone, E. 1982. Systematicity and attention
    in interlanguage. Language Learning. 32.
    69 - 84.

Varonis, E. and S. Gass.   In press.   Miscommunica-
    tion in native/non-native conversation.
    Language in Society.   14.2.
Zobl, H.   1980.   Developmental and transfer
    errors: Their common bases and (possibly)
    differential effects on subsequent learn-
    ing.   TESOL Quarterly.   14.   469 - 479.
Zobl, H.   1985.   Grammars in search of
    input and intake.   In S. Gass and C.
    Madden (eds.), Input in Second Language
    Acquisition.   Rowley, Mass.:   Newbury
    House.